Table of Contents (2012 Ed syllabus)

m

The role of PSP

In the practical real world a PSP may be a security manager, an external consultant, or a law enforcement agent. For purpose of the exam, however, you want to position yourself as a hired consultant – one who acts as an advisor to the company management. The company is your client, and you are helping it out. You advise, you guide, and you recommend.

You need to understand your client. If your client is absolutely new to security, full scale interviews and statistical analysis on crimes may be necessary. However, if your client has a working security mechanism in place, then you should conduct assessment basing primarily on inputs from management. In other words, management determines the depth and scope of the security project. Management makes the decisions. You suggest ways to improve, then carry out the decisions made by management. **You don't normally make decisions for your client.**

NOTE:

It is safe to say that you assume the role of project manager for your client's security project.

The security project would start by discussing the scope of work with your client. The most important meeting between you and the client would be the initial goal setting and policy review meeting. Senior management is going to get involved, and you are going to act as the facilitator. From this meeting you become aware of the level of risk your client is willing to assume and accept. Your work would then start from there.

When working on a project it is important to understand the background and operation of the client. You also want to know what you are up against. Protection against vandalism is totally different from protection against terrorist attack.

A PSP is more on the planning and design side of security. A security guard professional, on the other hand, is to provide client with professional protective services. A PSP needs not be a security guard. In fact, there are other certifications specially designed for the security guard profession, such as the CPO certification.

NOTE: **Formal definition of "security guard":** for example, in the New York state a Security Guard shall mean a person, other than a police officer, employed by a security guard company to principally perform functions that may include:

a.) protection of individuals and/or property from harm, theft or other unlawful activity;

b.) deterrence, observation, detection and/or reporting of incidents in order to prevent any unlawful or unauthorized activity including but not limited to unlawful or unauthorized intrusion or entry, larceny, vandalism, abuse, arson or trespass on property;

c.) street patrol service;

d.) response to but not installation or service of a security system alarm installed and/or used to prevent or detect unauthorized intrusion, robbery, burglary, theft, pilferage and other losses and/or to maintain security of a protected premises.

In order for your security measures to be effective, the security staff must always be helpful and patient with the regular staff. People tend to resist changes, so patience and understanding would be helpful as new security systems are being developed. Keep in mind, a Security Professional would often have to take the role of a salesman.

Physical Security Risk Management, Threat & Impact Assessment

What is Risk Management?

"Risk is a concept that auditors and managers use to express their concerns about the probable effects of an uncertain environment. Because the future cannot be predicted with certainty, auditors and managers have to consider a range of possible events that could take place"[1].

"Risk management is a discipline for dealing with uncertainty"[2].

As mentioned by David McNamee in his article "Management Control Concepts", uncertainty and randomness exist in nature, that risk is not something to be worried or concerned about but something to be managed. In fact, managing a range of risks is required for both survival and success in nowadays environment.

The discipline of risk management aims at helping an organization to identify, assess and control risks that may be present in operations, service delivery, staffing, and governance activities.

> **NOTE:** Risk in the context of security refers to the potential for realization of unwanted, adverse consequences to human life, health, property, or the environment.
>
> Every organization can and should use risk management strategies and tools to protect vital assets. Good risk management can reduce legal costs and lawsuit altogether. Remember, legal cost is one of the worst nightmares an organization can ever have.

---

[1] http://www.mc2consulting.com/riskart2.htm

[2] http://www.nonprofitrisk.org/tutorials/rm_tutorial/2.htm

The Risk Management Process

The risk management process provides a framework for identifying risks and deciding what to do about them. Since not all risks are created equal, risk management does not simply identify risks but also to weigh various risks and make decisions about which risks deserve immediate attention.

Faced with risk, the typical strategic choices include:

- Terminate the activity giving rise to risk

- Transfer risk to another party

- Reduce risk by using of appropriate control measures or mechanisms

- Accept the risk

NOTE: You need to understand the level of security risks your client is willing to accept. You may provide help in determining the acceptable risk level. You do want to ensure the assigned risk levels are clearly defined in a policy statement so that your work can be properly done with a basis to follow. An example policy statement may look something like:

"All full time staff must wear ID badges when staying in the office building".

Important: If you reasonably should know that crime around your facility may pose a risk and some elements of your facility may encourage a crime, you must address this in a very serious manner. This is all about concern on liability.

The risk management steps

The steps involved in proper risk management shall include:

o Context establishment - begin a risk management program by setting goals and identifying any potential barriers or impediments to the implementation of the program.

o Risks identification - categorize risks according to the major categories of assets of the organization in question.

o Risks evaluation and prioritization - establish a list of risk related action items in priority order.

o Strategies selection and implementation – use risk management techniques to address virtually every risk your organization is facing. Such techniques should include:

❖ Avoidance - do not offer programs that pose too great a risk.

❖ Modification – modify an activity to make it safer for all involved.

❖ Retention - make conscious decisions to retain risk.

❖ Sharing - share risk with another organization through contractual arrangement, such as insurance contracts and risk management service contracts.

o Program update – keep the risk management techniques and plans periodically reviewed and updated to make certain that they remain the most appropriate strategy.

Risk Management and Security

In order to properly identify and manage security risks, the security professional should aid in the following tasks:

- Develop a systematic, analytical and continuous risk management process.

- Ensure that risk identification, analysis and mitigation activities are integrated into life cycle processes.

- Apply risk identification and analysis methods.

- Define strategies and prioritize options to mitigate risk to levels acceptable to the organization.

- Report significant changes in risk to appropriate levels of management on both a periodic and event-driven basis.

 NOTE: **BCP is closely related to Risk Management.**

Business continuity is a term that describes the processes and procedures an organization puts in place to ensure that essential functions can continue during and after a disaster. Business continuity planning seeks to prevent interruption of mission-critical services, and to reestablish full functioning as swiftly and smoothly as possible.

The Risk Assessment Flow

 NOTE: From a physical security point of view, a risk assessment refers to a systematic analysis of the facilities assets and an assessment of the vulnerability of those assets from different types of threats.

Risk assessment is a process you can use to identify and evaluate risks and their potential effects. The first step to consider when preparing your risk assessment is to estimate the potential losses to which a business is exposed. The objective of the loss potential estimate is to identify critical aspects of the business operation and to place a monetary value on the loss estimate.

 NOTE: Criteria for the design of security systems should always be based on identification of critical business assets that may become potential targets and threat that are related to those assets.

The second step of the risk analysis is to evaluate the threats to the business. The third step in the risk analysis is to combine the estimates of the value of potential loss and probability of loss to develop an estimate of annual loss expectancy (ALE). The purpose is to pinpoint the significant threats as a guide to the selection of security measures and to develop a yardstick for determining the amount of money that is reasonable to spend on each of them.

 NOTE: In order to prepare for proper risk assessment, it is important that you have the right people to list the assets. They should be those who are familiar with the assets of the facility.

Quantitative means and qualitative means (NEW TOPIC)

Quantitative Risk Assessment is a formal and systematic approach for identifying events, estimating the likelihood and consequences of those events, and expressing the results as risk, in quantifiable units. The method typically includes things like:

● In-depth analysis of the severity and consequence of scenarios

● Predicted number of damages for each scenario

● Individual risk

- Group risk

- Potential losses

- Location specific risk

- Preventative and mitigation measures

- Sensitivity of results to the various uncertainties and assumptions

Quantitative analysis can present data in a manner which is friendlier for management (as it often expresses percentages, values, and probabilities due to the statistical nature of analysis). Qualitative risk analysis relies more on expert opinions and human inputs (such as interviews), therefore may produce results that are more subjective. The analysis may still have to involve some very basic calculations though.

Loss event analysis and cost/benefit analysis (NEW TOPIC)

Loss Event Probability aims to measure the number of ways in which a loss event can occur. Loss Event Criticality Rating refers to the assignment of letter and numerical ratings to each loss event or threat.

In any case, the security countermeasures shouldn't cost more than the benefits that can be received. Therefore, before spending $ to introduce new countermeasures one should first measure the return on the expenditures (ROE). This can be done through determining the avoided losses (AL), the recoveries made (R), and the cost of the security program (CSP). Remember this formula: AL+R / CSP = ROE.

Total cost of ownership (NEW TOPIC)

When assessing the cost of countermeasures, you need to know that on top of the product costs there are also other costs involved, such as:

- installation cost

- maintenance cost

- training cost

- repair cost

- operating cost

- cost of owning and running it …

The Total Cost of Acquisition (TCA) is a managerial accounting concept which aims to cover all the costs that are associated with buying goods, services, or assets.

Risk VS Threat and Vulnerability (NEW TOPIC)

The traditional definition of risk:

Risk is the product of threat and vulnerability. This model of risk is appropriate for assets where applicable threat data can be well predicted from historical events. One way to represent this is:

$$\text{Risk} = \text{Threat} \times \text{Vulnerability}$$

NOTE: Note that this model of risk assumes that we have knowledge of our vulnerabilities and our threats.

Threat is typically defined as an event (such as a flood, tornado, computer virus outbreak …etc.) of low probability yet highly damaging that really catches your attention. The chance of the event occurring is a probability that the event has happened. There is no time constraint, and the event will likely happen over some defined period of time. Security threats are typically described based on possible type of adversary and severity of attack; anticipated tactics, and the likelihood of attack.

NOTE: A common threat to many facilities is property loss. Other threats may include theft, violence, unauthorized access, lost persons and environmental hazards. Facilities highly visible to protest groups or terrorist groups are always subject to the threat of environmental hazards, such as chemical or biological poisoning of air, water or food.

Natural threats to a facility may include other disasters such as fire, flood, tornadoes, hurricanes and earthquakes.

Threat from criminals may include theft, burglary, vandalism, sabotage, arson, and embezzlement. They seek to take the assets for their own gain or satisfaction. Threat from Terrorists is different - the intent of terrorists is to disrupt operations through destroying the assets. Activists whose protests could also pose a threat through activities designed to halt production.

In any case, the analysis of potential threats should be based upon data. Different types of threat have different sources of data. For criminal threats the Uniform Crime Report is one good source of data.

As a security professional you need to understand that protective measures against high-level threats may or may not provide sufficient protection against low-level threats, that's why you would want to consider all types of threats during a threat assessment. After all, protective measures usually differ for each type of threat regardless of severity level.

Neal (1996) classified threats into different levels. At THREAT LEVEL 1 there is one or more unskilled individuals with little or no knowledge of security systems or physical protective measures, who launch the attack with little advanced planning, mostly targeting items with little or no security measures. At THREAT LEVEL 2 there are semi-skilled individuals with some (some only) knowledge of and ability to compromise low-level security systems. At THREAT LEVEL 3 there is a group of pretty skillful individuals who have strong motivations and capability in defeating the implemented security measures. At THREAT LEVEL 4 you are dealing with professionals who have extremely strong motivation and capabilities in using state of the art technology for launching attacks.

NOTE: In the security industry, the formal technical definition of Threat Assessment is the evaluation of threats based upon numerous characteristics such as history, magnitude of a threat, and capability of the entity or individual seeking to carry out the threat.

Design Basis Threat (DBT) is a concept that provides the information necessary for designing a physical protective system to detect and delay an attack for the most probable adversary. The DBT has a potentially significant impact on the cost and complexity of a physical security program. Therefore, identification of the DBT should be regarded as a major management decision that requires the input of various operational and management level personnel.

Vulnerability, on the other hand, is usually defined as a weakness that is exploited in some very negative way by the threat.

NOTE: There are other technical definitions of the term "vulnerability". The term could mean a characteristic of a critical infrastructure's design, management, or operation that renders the infrastructure susceptible to incapacitation by a threat. It could refer to a flaw in security procedures or

> operation that may affect normal business operation. It could also mean any weakness that may be exploited by an aggressor.

Vulnerability assessment characterizes and prioritizes business assets that may be targeted, evaluates where they are vulnerable, how they are currently protected, as well as the consequences of a successful attack, while Criticality analysis assesses a business function's security vulnerability based on its criticality to the organization's overall business objectives. In other words, once critical assets are identified, they should be characterized with respect to their attractiveness to various types of attack attempts, and then be prioritized basing on their criticality.

NOTE: In the security industry, the formal technical definition of Vulnerability Assessment is the evaluation of characteristics that contribute to and mitigate the susceptibility of an asset to damage or weakness that can be exploited by an aggressor.

Through a comprehensive vulnerability assessment you achieve the following:

- characterize and prioritize assets that may be targeted

- evaluate assets that are vulnerable to attack and find out how they are currently protected as well as the consequences of successful attacks

Developing a vulnerability assessment would involve defining a list of vulnerabilities and potential improvements that are properly ranked according to the potential risk. In other words you start by reviewing all the physical threats, then characterize and prioritize assets that may be targeted and find out how they are currently protected as well as the consequences of successful attacks.

You may rely on a Physical Vulnerability Survey to help building up such a list and arrive at a thorough assessment of physical security. As an example, to estimate the Physical

Security potential in the greater area where the facility is located (the county level or the city level), the survey may consider:

● Prominent Types of Businesses

● Socio-Economic Profile

● Overall Crime Rate

● Violent Crime Rate

● Ratio of Private-Public-Commercial Property

● Presence of Gangs and Gang Related Activities

To estimate the Physical Security potential in the immediate area (at the street corner level), the survey may consider:

● Specific types of businesses in the area

● Ratio of Private-Public-Commercial properties

● Special entities in area

● Walk-in traffic

● Locations of Police Station and Fire Station

To estimate the Physical Security potential within the building area, the survey may consider:

● Size/shape of parking lot(s)

● Outside lighting on building(s) and in parking lot(s) and walkways

● View unobstructed from parking to building entrances

- Area secured by fencing

- Access control to parking

- Security personnel present

- Opening hours

- Number of building entrances

- Electronic security on outer doors

- Exterior / interior roof access

> **NOTE:** Physical security perimeters are usually expressed in the form of concentric circles surrounding each asset, with each succeeding circle widening (and with progressively lower levels of security). You should make use of floor plans and plot plans for identifying assets that are to be protected.

With such a list handy you may contemplate what level of protection is acceptable and how many of the recommendations should be considered for implementation. This is when a cost-benefit analysis should come into play. In fact, security improvements may best be prioritized through comparing the cost to implement a measure against the degree of risk reduction that the measure could ideally provide.

> **NOTE:** A cost-benefit analysis would be most robust if the relevant benefits can be readily quantified, and would be less effective when benefits cannot be easily converted to monetary terms.

A vulnerability assessment for physical security must consider the routes and means used to attack and to protect the asset from attack. There is a need to find out how access can be gained to an asset and how that asset may be compromised. The consequences of a successful attack would accordingly be considered when weighing the cost and impact of implementing appropriate protective measures.

In some cases the consequences may simply not justify the investment to address a threat. You just have to know what is to be protected behind the door and determine if it is going to worth the security investment.

NOTE: Asset value is typically determined by considering the criticality of the asset for its user and/or others, how easily the asset can be replaced, as well as some measure of the asset's relative value.

The labor force of the facility is an asset. The corporate knowledge is also an asset.

For areas where access is highly infrequent, simple mechanism lock may just do the job well enough. Frankly, mechanism lock is way less expensive than its electronic counterpart and is usually more service-free. You want to use expensive electric lock only when you are implementing an access control system.

Legal concerns

A basic tenet of legal liability may compel an organization that is made aware of a condition to take reasonable steps to eliminate or mitigate a hazardous condition. A finding of negligence for damages stemming from a security breach would usually require reasonable ability to foresee the damages, a duty to the injured person and/or damaged properties, and actual violation of the duty proximately causing the injury and/or damage.

Once a vulnerability assessment is conducted, the resulting recommendations could well be considered as notice of a dangerous condition and could result in liability if the recommendations are not being properly attended to.

Identifying Risks

As said before, risk in the context of security refers to the potential for realization of unwanted, adverse consequences to human life, health, property, or the environment. The key part of the risk management process is the assessment of the potential risks to the business which could result from disasters or emergency situations. You MUST consider ALL the possible incidents and the impact that follows. Examples of the risks that are possible for any organization on earth include (and not limited to):

o   Environmental Disasters

o   Deliberate Disruption (e.g. terrorist attack)

o   Loss of Utilities and Services

o   Equipment or System Failure

o   Serious Security Breaches

 NOTE: Identification and characterization of business assets that are related to these risks are ALWAYS based on consideration of the mission and the resources required for performance.

Loss Calculations

The 3 major models are:

● Single Loss Expectancy (SLE)

● Annualized Loss Expectancy (ALE)

● Cumulative Loss Expectancy (CLE)

The Single Loss Expectancy model is the model upon which the Annualized Loss Expectancy and Cumulative Loss Expectancy models are based. This simple (and less accurate) model has its roots in accounting, with the purpose of determining how much value in terms of dollars will be lost, and is often used to express the results in a financial impact analysis.

The Annualized Loss Expectancy Model of risk comes closer (relatively) to painting an accurate picture of risk by adding the probability of an event happening over a single year's time. To reach an answer, you need to first calculate the Single Loss Expectancy to determine this value. Then you obtain the product of the Single Loss Expectancy and the value of the asset to produce the Annualized Loss Expectancy. The formula looks like this:

Single Loss Expectancy	x	Annualized Rate of Occurrence	=	Annualized Loss Expectancy

The Cumulative Loss Model approaches risks by taking into account all of the bad things that are likely to happen to your business over the next year. You will need to look at each threat, the probability of each threat against your business, and then derive an expected loss. You can take all of the threats, and compute the annual rate of each threat occurring.

Regardless of how you calculate your risk and losses, at the end of the day cost effectiveness must be given serious consideration. Remember, reducing all components of a risk to low could be highly impractical. Rather than attempting to reduce all risks to low, you may better off implementing improvements that reduce risk to all critical facilities to medium. The resources saved could be better spent on somewhere else.

Business Impact Analysis

The BIA is an evaluation of the strengths and weaknesses of your company's disaster preparedness and the impact an interruption would have on your business. Every BIA should include an exploratory component to reveal any vulnerabilities, and a planning component to develop strategies for minimizing risk. A well done BIA should be capable of identifying costs linked to failures, such as loss of cash flow, replacement of equipment, salaries paid to catch up with a backlog of work, and loss of profits …etc.

The result of analysis is a business impact analysis report, which describes the potential risks specific to the organization studied. It should quantify the importance of business components and suggest appropriate fund allocation for measures to protect them. The possibilities of failures are likely to be assessed in terms of their impacts on safety, finances, marketing, legal compliance, and quality assurance.

As part of the risk assessment effort, business impact analysis has 3 primary goals:

- Criticality Prioritization: Critical business units must be identified and prioritized.

- Downtime Escalation: Estimate the maximum tolerable downtime.

- Resource Requirements: Identify resource requirements for the critical processes.

Business impact analysis generally involves 4 steps:

1. Gathering the needed assessment materials

2. The vulnerability assessment

3. Analyzing the information compiled

4. Documenting the results and presenting recommendations to management.

Preparing for internal threats

Most threats are from internal sources. Therefore, you should get your HR people involved in the security planning effort. You may want to enforce the practice of doing background checks of job applicants. Generally speaking, such background checks should include confirming past employment, education, professional certifications, and references, plus facts available through public records.

 NOTE: It is important for background checks to get completed prior to job offers are being made. Additionally, background checks with periodic reviews should be conducted for current employees whenever possible.

Corresponding applications for employment must accordingly include a waiver whereby the applicant allows the background check and authorizes his former employers to speak with your HR people. For job positions that are highly "sensitive" you may want to expand the background check to include criminal and other records such as military service, credit history, and even character references.

> **NOTE:** Background check results can turn out to be faulty so you may want to have them confirmed through other channels.

High level security programs are complex programs that may include the use of physical security systems plus working in or near serious, significant materials that may pose a threat to human life and the environment. For these programs to work a background check must first be conducted. Complete honesty and integrity on the part of the employees are highly emphasized.

Depending on the nature, size and complexity of a business operation, the use of employee identification (ID) badges may be a good idea. ID badges provide instant verification of individuals, and color-coded badges can effectively alert others if the individuals are in an inappropriate area.

> **NOTE:** **Badges are an important security tool for identifying persons.**
>
> The decision to have employees wear badges is one effective way to upgrade security. A badge allows one to quickly identify whether a person is authorized to access an area. This would be particularly useful in a large facility with multiple areas and varying levels of security.
>
> Photo badges can act as an effective deterrent to unsophisticated intruders and the general public. They will not deter a sophisticated intruder though.

All employees (including temporary and part-time employees) should be issued ID badges and should be required to wear them at all times. Temporary ID badges may be occasionally issued but they should be made time-sensitive or light-sensitive so that their nature can be visibly apparent. When necessary, authorized personnel must escort employees and/or guests who are visiting locations outside of their authorized areas.

 NOTE: You may want to compartmentalize access to various parts of your facility such that only those necessary personnel would be granted access to the relevant specific areas.

Very importantly, you should provide your staff with a clear protocol for reporting security concerns. This procedure can be as simple as a phone number to the relevant manager or a detailed procedure for notifying the security department. The bottom line is, your staff must know what to do when there is a need to report anything security related.

Preparing for emergency response

You will need to take into account the various stakeholders in an emergency response scenario. Below are the stakeholders that will most likely be involved:

● Internal (corporate and business unit level) groups

● External groups (customers, vendors, suppliers, public, INSURANCE COMPANIES)

● External agencies (local, state, national governments, emergency responders, regulators, etc.)

● Media (print, radio, television, Internet)

Important points to remember regarding the arrangement with these stakeholders for handling emergencies shall include:

- A list of important contacts must be maintained all the time by several key people in the organization. One of these key people must be available off-site (imagine what can happen if all the key people get buried in the destructed building).

- Determine the chain of command structure – who should be in charge if, let's say, the president may never be available again?

- Each business unit should have at least one person assigned to keep a list of contacts of all the staff within the unit – during a tragedy there is a need to find out who is still missing. There is also a need to keep the family members of the staff fully informed on what is happening.

- A crisis communication plan must always be in place. Communications must be properly maintained with the outside world during the tragedy. You will need help from various external agencies. In fact, get in touch with these agencies regularly to determine how you all can work together in the case of emergency. You will also want to let your customers know that everything is under control and there is no need for them to worry too much.

- It will be very ugly if the person in charge of the organization is the last one who is informed of the tragedy. When something goes wrong, the CEO is often the target of the media. Do NOT upset the media. Do NOT upset the reporters.

 NOTE: 800 MHz radios are commonly used by fire and police departments, therefore you should have at least one 800 MHz radio to facilitate communication in the case of emergency.

In order to enable an organization to respond to and recovery from disruptive and destructive information security events, the security professional should aid in the planning and performance of the following tasks:

- Develop and implement process for detecting, identifying and analyzing security-related events

- Develop response and recovery plans that include organizing, training and equipping the teams

- Ensure periodic testing of the response and recovery plans where appropriate

- Ensure the execution of response and recover plans as required

- Establish procedures for documenting an event as a basis for subsequent action including forensics when necessary

- Manage post-event reviews to identify causes and corrective actions

It is recommended that a number of different mechanisms be employed to detect security-related events. The information gathered through the detection process should be assembled and organized to identify security-related events. This identification process may take place using a criteria defined by the security manager or by following industry best practices. In any case, by categorizing and prioritizing security events, quick action can take place on the important security events without getting lost.

The security professional should meet with local and federal emergency management officials to understand what governmental capabilities exist. Most countries and governments have emergency management agencies that can advise and assist the population in dealing with a wide range of natural and man-made threats.

Responding to incidents and managing recovery

The typical incident response goals are:

- Recovering quickly and efficiently from security incidents

- Minimizing impact of the security incident

- Responding systematically and decreasing the likelihood of reoccurrence

- Balancing operation and security

- Dealing with legal issues

To effectively plan for security specific Incident Handling, you may want to follow the steps below:

1. Come up with a clear, concise statement of scope, intention and constraints.

2. Provide business resource descriptions.

3. Perform an impact assessment.

4. Delegate roles and responsibilities (you can't do it all).

5. List staff and vendor contact information (in case you need outside help).

6. Be specific about your incident response actions, notifications and priorities.

7. Identify the necessary essential response resources.

8. Spell out incident investigation and documentation requirements.

9. Continually exercise, update and maintain your plan.

One critical part of handling any serious emergency situation is in the management of the Disaster Recovery Phase. Remember, the priority during recovery is ALWAYS the safety and well being of the employees and other involved persons. Other priorities include the minimization of the emergency itself, the removal or minimization of the threat of further injury or damage and the re-establishment of external services (power, telecom …etc).

The Business Recovery Phase will then follow directly on from the Disaster Recovery Phase. This Phase involves the restoration of normal business operations. On the other hand, preventions against disasters may be implemented in many forms, and may make your life significantly easier during and after a disaster. Examples:

●   You may use surge protectors to minimize the effect of power surges.

●   You may use Uninterruptible Power Supply (UPS) to ensure continuous supply of power.

- You may set up more fire alarms and make the extinguishers more easily accessible.

- You may purchase insurance coverage on company assets.

Testing the plan

The effectiveness of any plan you have for emergency situations can only be assessed if rigorous testing is carried out in realistic conditions. Therefore, the plan should be tested within a realistic environment with simulating conditions applicable in an actual emergency. All persons who will be involved with recovering a particular business process during emergency should be REQUIRED to participate in the testing process.

Plan maintenance

In today's world, the pace of change will never slow down but will continue to increase. It is necessary for the plan to keep pace with these changes in order for it to be useful in the event of a disruptive emergency.

Be realistic...

When having limited resources you must do your best to make the most from low-cost/high-value security options rather than struggling for unlikely funding on major infrastructure countermeasures. Not every door has to be controlled, nor is it always necessary to be under 24-hour monitoring...

 NOTE: As a matter of fact, you may find simple operational changes very cost-effective in enhancing physical security.

Security System Planning & Design

A-B-C-D Planning

You plan facility protection to ensure both the integrity of operations and the security of assets. Planning is important due to the fact that modification of security measures after occupying a facility can be costly and highly impractical. In fact, location of a facility should be well planned prior to thinking about any protection measures.

When planning security, you may want to reference the A B C D method.

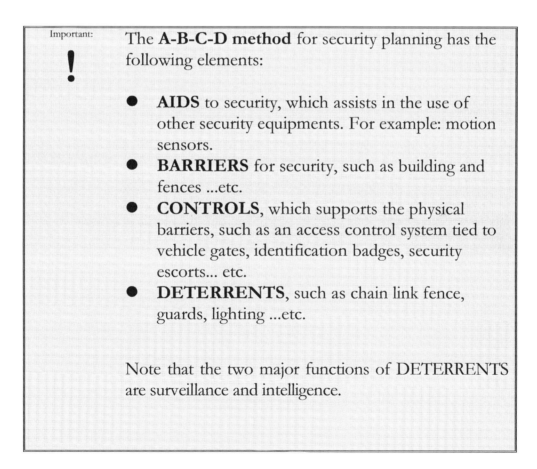

Important:

!

The **A-B-C-D method** for security planning has the following elements:

- **AIDS** to security, which assists in the use of other security equipments. For example: motion sensors.
- **BARRIERS** for security, such as building and fences ...etc.
- **CONTROLS**, which supports the physical barriers, such as an access control system tied to vehicle gates, identification badges, security escorts... etc.
- **DETERRENTS**, such as chain link fence, guards, lighting ...etc.

Note that the two major functions of DETERRENTS are surveillance and intelligence.

At the same time, you have to realize that the goal of implementing any security system design is to allow the security force to cover more area and do more in less time. The trend is for the security force to focus more on response but less on D D D (deterrence, detection and delay). Therefore, you do a good job so that D D D can be achieved by design, and the security force can concentrate more on response.

> **NOTE:** Keep in mind, no matter how advanced an access-control system is, it would be no better than its weakest link. Basing on experience, the weakness link seems to be PEOPLE ....

The concept of IPS

An Integrated physical security (IPS) consists of three mutually supporting elements, which are physical security measures, operational procedures and policies. Physical security covers all devices and technologies for perimeter protection. Operational procedures cover how the facility works on a day-to-day business. Policies define who does what and the actions to take for preventing attack or incident.

> **NOTE:** A multi-step process to implement IPS has been suggested, which is DDDRRR – deterrence, detection, delay, response, recovery and re-evaluation.

Facility Design

You must check geographical factors carefully. Whenever possible, avoid having your facilities located near high crime and high traffic areas. Always take into account approach routes, traffic patterns, and nearby transportation. At the facility site, keep the number of separate buildings to a minimum. Do not have them grouped too close together.

Facility entrances should be kept to a minimum commensurate with fire safety, access control and crime prevention. Convenience of access must be considered, but single entrance with multiple interior routes is usually more preferable to several outside entrances.

All entrances must be planned with sufficient guard posts, access control systems and procedures. Additionally, reception desks, barriers, and other controls should be planned from the start.

> **Important:** ❗ If a facility is surrounded by a fence, the main entrance should have a guard post with phone and radio communication equipments ready. Regular communication with the officer there has to be maintained.

> **Important:** ❗ For project on existing facility, the first step in determining the status of a facility's existing security system would be to determine the type and function of that facility. Upgrade of the existing security system may then be accordingly planned.
>
> Proper design documentation should start with marking the facility floor plan and/or plot plan. In other words, you must devise a plan that can fit with the existing facility layout (you just don't have the option of redesigning the facility).

FEMA recommendation

The Federal Emergency Management Agency (FEMA) recommended that facilities place limit on the number of doors that are used regularly for entering and exiting a building while still providing sufficient emergency exits. It was recommended that hollow steel or steel-clad doors with steel frames be used for security application, or blast-resistant doors be deployed for high-risk facilities.

> **NOTE:** Doors should be located in well-lighted area that can be easily seen. If steel based door is not an option, use door made of aluminum alloy or solid-core hardwood. Double doors should be secured with multiple-point long flush bolts. Door hinges should not use removable pins. If glass doors are required, have them fully framed and equipped with burglar-resistant tempered glass. Glass doors are good in the sense that they do not conceal inappropriate activity (while recessed doorways do).

In any case the strength of the latch and frame anchor should equal that of the door and frame, as it is believed that the weakest part of most door assemblies is the latching component.

> **NOTE:** As recommended by FEMA, exterior doors should open outward and hinges should be on a door's interior. Keep in mind, exterior doors should not need handles and locks on the outside. They should have as little exposed hardware as possible.

Door modifications

Along your project effort you may need to upgrade some door openings to receive mortised electrified hardware. Note that doing so would be more difficult than installing surface-applied electrified hardware since you would need to remove the existing door internals and replace them with new internal, prewired conduit preparations. Additionally, you would quite likely have to retrofit the door frame to receive an electrified transfer hinge.

A magnetic or punched keycard-operated lockset would be easier to install and configure. They typically use lock bodies that fit most existing mortise-lock preparations. Since they are battery-powered there would be no need for hard wiring. Do keep in mind, surface application of these locks could restrict the swing of an existing door to only one direction...

Utility connections

Incoming site utilities (power, water, gas ...etc) need to be protected from accidental or deliberate damage. You should have the core site utility connections entering the site and facility properly hardened. Exposed pipelines should be protected. Electrical lines should be placed underground. Redundant utility connection sources should be provided whenever possible.

Accessibility and safety concern

Accessibility of entrances for individuals with disabilities must receive proper attention. ALSO, safety and fire protection requirements must be incorporated in the construction plan.

NOTE: With the Americans with Disabilities Act there has to be an area in a multi-story building that is designated an "area of rescue assistance." This should be an area near the exit stairway. The area should have expanded space for the disabled persons to wait for rescue when the building needs to be rapidly evacuated. There has to be signage plus two-way communication with the ground.

Means of egress from a protected area must be clearly defined and established. The fire department would have to make sure you do....

> **Important:**
> **!**
> A security design for a facility must comply with local building codes and fire codes. For a facility in the US the design must also comply with the Americans with Disabilities Act (ADA) guidelines.

> **Important:**
> **!**
> For projects on new facilities, you may need to have a fire protection plan in place. Or, as a minimum, your security design plan must be compatible with the fire protection plan.
>
> A proper fire protection plan should identify all the horizontal and vertical fire separations by hourly rate and show all fire fighting access, sprinkled areas, exit conditions and distances. In facilities where security and appearance are important, extinguisher cabinets may be provided.

OSHA (Occupational Health and Safety Act) compliance may also require your attention, even though concerns are mostly on Lead Based Paint and Asbestos Surveys, not on security measures.

Space configuration

You should locate offices or other facilities in close proximity, preferably on the same or successive floors. Always try to locate sensitive operations away from entrances.

Utility systems must be protected against unauthorized access. Protection of phone and electrical closets and conduit runs, heating and cooling systems, water supplies ...etc must all be carefully considered. Special emphasis must be placed on security systems and safeguards when constructing facilities for sensitive activities. And, a contingency plan must be developed to protect personnel and property in the event of emergencies.

Door Detail Schedule

When conducting a Vulnerability Survey you will need to record information in a Door Detail Schedule (DDS). This DDS is a document that describes all door equipments necessary for making a physical security system operational. It should cover all openings and you must ensure proper naming is in place so that everyone is referring to the same thing.

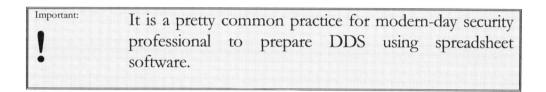

Important:	It is a pretty common practice for modern-day security professional to prepare DDS using spreadsheet software.

Design that involves protecting high tech equipments

If your facility is hosting high tech computer equipments, consider the following as the elements of a minimum protection level:

- Servers must be protected by backup and offsite data storage. The offsite storage of backup media must be housed in a secure facility.
- Uninterruptible Power Supply (UPS) supporting all servers and essential peripheral equipments should be deployed.
- A climate controlled environment separate from the building HVAC, (dedicated air conditioning with in-room temperature controls) should be implemented. High tech computer equipments require reliable climate control at all times.
- Cooling and electrical capacity must be planned and monitored for outages.
- Secured access to the facility with documentation listing all individuals who currently have access and monitoring/auditing of ingress/egress via CCTV and the like must be enforced.
- Servers in the facility must require authentication for local access and must not be left logged in while unattended.

- There should be the capability to quickly change "access codes" if personnel changes warrant. Access codes must be changed periodically.
- Automated fire detection and suppression systems must be in place.

Design specification documents

Design specifications may be divided into three major parts, which are General, Products, and Execution. The General section has information and provisions (mainly administrative provisions) of the specifications that are not product specific. The Products section covers product specific information. The Execution section covers in-depth information on the function and installation of the design.

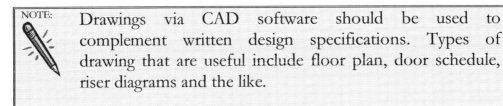

NOTE: Drawings via CAD software should be used to complement written design specifications. Types of drawing that are useful include floor plan, door schedule, riser diagrams and the like.

Security Analysis, Survey & Inspection

Crime Analysis

Crime is an important element of hazard identification which helps in justifying the allocation of security resources. **This has to be done.** Crime Analysis may be defined as a set of systematic, analytical processes directed at providing timely and pertinent information relative to crime patterns and trend correlations to assist in planning the deployment of resources for the prevention and suppression of criminal activities, aiding the investigative process, and increasing apprehensions and the clearance of cases. ADMINISTRATIVE analysis deals with long-range comparisons, such as quarterly, semi-annually or annually. STRATEGIC analysis deals with operational strategies and seeks solutions to on-going problems. TACTICAL analysis deals with immediate criminal offenses.

Physical security survey

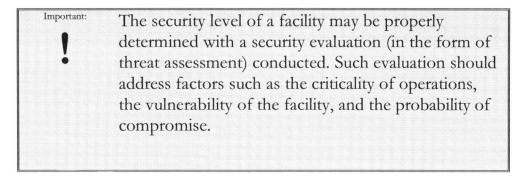

Important:

! The security level of a facility may be properly determined with a security evaluation (in the form of threat assessment) conducted. Such evaluation should address factors such as the criticality of operations, the vulnerability of the facility, and the probability of compromise.

A physical security survey is necessary for determining the security level of the facility and the minimum-security safeguards required for protecting personnel and assets.

- First there is a need for an initial physical security survey prior to constructing, leasing, acquiring, modifying, or occupying a facility or area to determine the minimum-security safeguards required.

- Then you need a follow-up physical security survey prior to acceptance of the property or occupancy to ensure the completion of required modifications and/or security upgrades if applicable.

- You will need to have periodic reassessments of facilities conducted to ascertain whether your security program meets the required standards and/or regulations.

- To make things work smoothly, comprehensive and continuing awareness and education effort for gaining the interest and support of employees, contractors, consultants, and visitors would be needed.

- Finally, there must be procedures in place for taking immediate, positive, and orderly action to safeguard life and property during an emergency.

- If serious deficiency is found, a resurvey must be planned.

Initial Survey

An initial physical security survey should be conducted prior to constructing, leasing, acquiring, modifying, or occupying a facility or area. It should describe the kinds of modification required for raising the level of security commensurate with the levels of criticality and vulnerability.

Follow-up Survey

Follow-up survey should be conducted to ensure the completion of modifications as recommended in the initial physical security survey. In fact this survey should be conducted prior to the formal acceptance of the property.

Supplemental Survey

Supplemental survey should be conducted when changes in the organization, mission, facility, or the threat level of the facility alter or affect the facility's security posture.

Special Survey

Special survey should be conducted for examining specific issue related to specific incidents

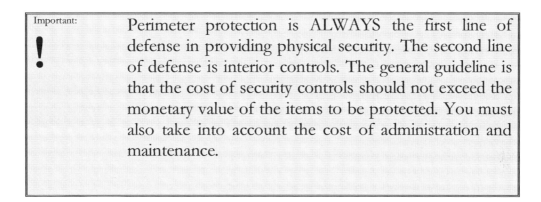

> **Important:**
>
> ! Perimeter protection is ALWAYS the first line of defense in providing physical security. The second line of defense is interior controls. The general guideline is that the cost of security controls should not exceed the monetary value of the items to be protected. You must also take into account the cost of administration and maintenance.

It would be helpful to start your physical survey by following a facility walk-through schedule, with the relevant site plan and/or floor plan as your guide. You may want to begin at the main entrance, then focus on those openings and areas that are the most active and heavily used.

Security inspection

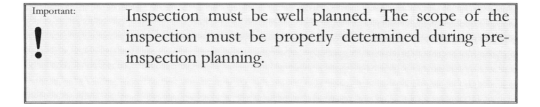

> **Important:**
>
> ! Inspection must be well planned. The scope of the inspection must be properly determined during pre-inspection planning.

Inspections may be announced or unannounced and are usually conducted for determining the extent of compliance with security regulations or procedures. Frequency of inspections should be based on the criticality and vulnerability of the facility or the level of classification or value of information processed at a facility. Generally speaking, the types of Inspections may include:

Evaluative inspection

This is sort of a fact-finding inspection which is generally positive in tone and is aimed at promoting liaison and security awareness while taking a broad, general look at a facility. Deficiencies when found may be resolved either on the spot or within a non-specified time frame, may be noted and recommendations for further corrective actions to be taken.

Compliance inspection

Full compliance inspection is generally conducted for enforcement purposes. It focuses on compliance with the established standards and regulations. After-hours room check is also a form of compliance inspection.

Follow-up inspection

Follow-up inspection is also a form of compliance inspection. It is normally conducted to ensure that facility officials have complied with recommendations from the earlier inspections.

Self inspection

Self-inspection is usually initiated by the security officer or the facility manager to evaluate his/her own security program.

Closeout inspection

Closeout inspection is usually accomplished right before a faciity is administratively terminated. During closeout inspections, all areas and containers that have been authorized for the storage of confidential material must be checked to ensure proper and complete removal.

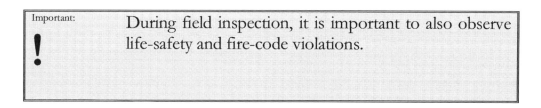

> **Important:**
> ❗ During field inspection, it is important to also observe life-safety and fire-code violations.

An inspection report should be produced after the completion of the inspection. The report should be distributed to the relevant parties in a timely manner and should require a response to any recommendations.

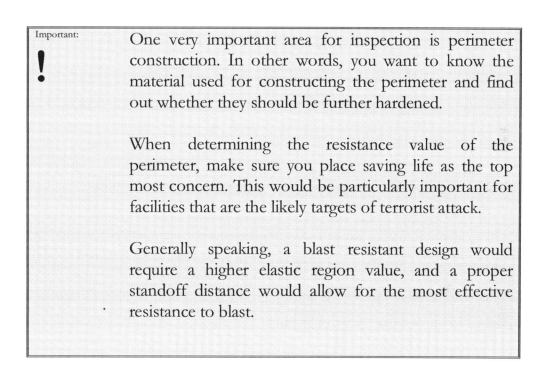

> **Important:**
> ❗ One very important area for inspection is perimeter construction. In other words, you want to know the material used for constructing the perimeter and find out whether they should be further hardened.
>
> When determining the resistance value of the perimeter, make sure you place saving life as the top most concern. This would be particularly important for facilities that are the likely targets of terrorist attack.
>
> Generally speaking, a blast resistant design would require a higher elastic region value, and a proper standoff distance would allow for the most effective resistance to blast.

Achieving proper balance

Given all sorts of real-world constraints, no security system can be completely effective against all kinds of potential threats and invasive actions. Since resources are finite, your design must be optimized in such a way that the performance goals can be successfully met within the specified limitations. A balanced approach that does not allocate all resources to any single aspect of the problem while ignoring another would be preferred.

Generally, there are three types of human adversaries that should be considered when designing a physical protection system. They are outsiders, insiders, and outsiders in collusion with insiders. They may use tactics of force, stealth, or deceit in achieving their wrongful goals. Adversary characteristics could be very different. This is why security systems to prevent theft and security systems to prevent sabotage (which would often include actions of vandalism) are often highly different.

Detection, delay, and response are the basic and most fundamental elements of a physical protection system. With these in mind when developing a security design, proper balance between hardware and procedural elements must be achieved. To be effective, physical protection should include policies and procedures designed to keep the physical protection systems functioning as intended.

NOTE: Always keep in mind, without staff commitment to the security program, your security program will never be effective. Integrating security into the culture of an organization is important. You do not expect a regular staff to become a security guard, but you should expect your full-time permanent staff force to possess the knowledge and awareness capability to detect, discern, and deny an outsider from causing an emergency situation within the organization.

Approaches to Physical Security

Generally speaking, the first step in implementing physical security is separating your assets from the threats. This would mean separating the property from the public, commonly done through fencing and access control. If it is not practical to separate the property, you may want to control some of the more critical assets within the property by physical separation inside. This is best done through separating areas within the facility and implementing secured doorways.

Assets Protection Principles & Planning

Assets may be classified as people, materials and property (physical and intellectual). A successful Assets Protection Program must address all these. Potential source of disruptions to operation of the assets may be internal or external. Internal sources of disruptions can include disgruntled employees and former employees. External sources can include disgruntled customers, disgruntled vendors and contractors; or someone who have no previous relationships at all. Accidents and disasters are also considered as sources of outside disruption.

For assets protection to be successful, the plan must be realistic, and top management support must be secured. Very importantly, the security plan must be based on the specific needs and resources of the organization of interest.

Plan Objectives & Elements

The plan must provide methods for responding to emergencies and minimizing the opportunities for disruptions to assets operations. It has to provide a systematic approach to security which covers the controlling, monitoring, and recording of access, events, and incidents. There should be a training program which increases employee awareness of the various security issues. Employee responsibilities with respect to security must also be clearly clarified.

A comprehensive yet systematic approach to security should include a vulnerability analysis, a careful selection and implementation of countermeasures, and a thorough testing program for validating the security plan. For all these to work, total commitment from all level of management is a MUST.

You want to realize that security issues often overlap with concerns addressed by Human Resources. Some examples include tardiness, substance abuse, violence and psychological problems. Improper activities of employees can also produce problems. Conflict of interest is usually the most common concern.

Vulnerability & Criticality Analysis

Vulnerability should be based on these variables:

- event profiles

- event probabilities

- event criticality

Event profiles are used to list all the potential threats. Event probability indicates which potential threats will likely become actual ones. A checklist can be used to call out specific pieces of information related to an event, such as type, time, and locations. A risk matrix can be used to compare two or more factors which can be very helpful for determining event probability. Criticality is a measure that assesses the impact an event occurrence may have on assets operations.

Talking about Criticality, a fatal level indicates possible discontinuance of operations. A very serious level means major negative impact on operations. A moderately serious level refers to noticeable negative impact. A marginally serious level means full recovery from impact is quite possible with the resources on hand.

Operational Testing

Ongoing testing effort is essential as it identifies risks which may still exist within the various operations. It can be used to isolate deficiencies within the existing system. It can also be used to identify where changes are required for the security system to meet growing demand. It can also provide a means of ensuring that security program policies and procedures are truly and adequately meeting the practical needs of operations.

Plan Perception

Every element of a successful security plan must be reviewed for its ability of loss prevention AND also for its ability to create the perception of a safe and secure environment. The perception of protection the plan presents is highly important.

Illusory Techniques

The use of illusory techniques may be preferable in some situations. By establishing the image of security (which requires an assessment of the types of illusions necessary) the overall costs of implementation can be lowered. For example, instead of using functional CCTV you may use simulated CCTV domes in some less important locations. Do realize that once an illusory technique has been compromised, it is going to have no further practical value and must be accordingly discontinued.

Security Product Standards

Underwriter Laboratories (UL) provides standards for security products. Security professionals should be familiar with the various applicable UL standards, in particular the standard 294 (Access Control Systems) and standard 1076 (Alarm Systems and Units, Proprietary Burglar).

Types of Incident Response

A successful assets protection plan must have clearly defined responses in place in the event of an incident. Responses should be balanced in their effect, and should be both preventative and punitive in nature. A preventative response is initiated before the unauthorized act. It is designed to serve as a clear warning that additional response will be initiated. A punitive response, on the other hand, is initiated once penetration has occurred or in progress. Its objective is the identification and apprehension of the perpetrator. Balanced response involves both of these responses, used either singularly or in combination throughout the response process.

Protection in depth

Layered security systems are built on the "protection in depth" principle, one that requires that an attacker defeat several protective barriers or security layers in order to accomplish its attack goal. The design implies that no matter how an attacker attempts to accomplish his goal, he is going to encounter the effective elements of your physical protection system.

 NOTE: An effective security layering approach would require that an attacker penetrate multiple, separate barriers in order to gain entry to a critical asset at a facility. This makes his life way more difficult and helps to ensure that the security system would remain effective in the event of a failure or an attacker bypassing any one layer of security.

Physical Security controls include the materials, equipment, and procedures that are used in securing a site. They are one element of an in-depth program of physical protection. Another component of a physical security system is the perception of security both on the part of authorized personnel on site and potential intruders.

For a physical security plan to be truly effective, all employees, customers, visitors and vendors must perceive that they are truly secure, that they must believe they are in a safe and secure environment.

Barriers

One major goal of in-depth protection is achieved by controlling access through the use of barriers. Barriers refer to any means one uses to control the flow of access to an area. They are typically arranged in concentric layers. The region which is the object of the protection is usually at the center, with the lowest level of security residing at the outermost layer. Each layer closer to this center region has a progressively higher level of security. The objective is to deter or delay the intruder.

Generally, there should be at least three layers of barrier protection, which are outer, middle and inner. The barriers define the physical limits of an area. Barriers may be either natural or artificial. Examples of natural barriers include bodies of water, mountains, marshes, deserts or other terrain. Structural barriers refer to those man-made entities like fences and walls.

The outer protective layer may have fencing, natural barriers, walls, lighting systems, signs, alarms …etc in place. These are controls that can define property lines and channeling personnel/ vehicles through the designated access points.

Exterior barriers should have two "clear zones", that is, one on either side of the barrier. Each zone should have 20 feet or more of open space. The purpose is to provide an unobstructed view of the barrier and its surrounding area.

The middle layer of barrier protection may begin at the exteriors of any buildings on the site. Security features that may be included here are lighting systems, alarm systems, locking devices, signs, and additional fencing. Generally, one should consider a building as a six-sided box. Barrier design should accordingly include provisions for protection from roof entry as well as intrusion from underground.

Building surfaces are typically not designed to be barriers even though they may deter penetration given proper design. One must realize that the most significant weakness in building surfaces as security barriers are those openings such as doors and windows.

The inner lay may also consist of several levels. It is the final barrier against intrusion.

A barrier can be compromised given enough time, money, personnel, planning, and imagination. Therefore, to help counter such threats, multiple barriers should be used. Also, they should be constructed with the understanding that additional countermeasures may be necessary for improving the barrier's capability.

Protective lighting

Protective lighting can have an active role in deterring intrusion. One factor in the effectiveness of lighting used this way is its brightness and position in relation to the intruder (the "glare effect"). There will be a disorienting effect and also a deterring effect when one suddenly fills an area with high levels of illumination triggered by an intrusion detection device. As a component of a lighting system design, this kind of effect can be enhanced by keeping an area in low light levels until an intruder is detected.

Lighting serves extremely well as a psychological deterrent.

Perimeter defense

The perimeter of the facility includes fence, access gates and the like that surround the site. The site sits between the perimeter and the buildings. The buildings and structures within a facility serve well as the next physical barrier for stopping intruders. You rely on building systems to protect your critical assets from intruders.

To provide multiple layers of defense, you should have perimeter intrusion detection mechanisms placed at the outer edges of the asset boundary, and delays should be located as close to the edge as possible. The goal is to allow the security system to generate an early alarm during an intrusion while delaying an attacker as he attempts to reach the intended target. In other words, a layered approach should start with the outer perimeter and goes inward to the facility site and finally to the contents of the buildings and the assets inside.

Unauthorized access surveillance system VS access-egress control system

With an unauthorized access surveillance system, detector sensors are typically installed near the fence or other barrier which marks the perimeter of the facility. When you have these sensors installed outdoors, special care must be taken in choosing the proper installation location. In areas with frequent snows or fog the sensors may experience problems processing images normally. There is also a need for confirming that all sensors are working properly. This can be done through a special system which performs checks on the sensors everyday.

On the other hand, an access-egress control system would have authentication devices such as ID card readers installed at the gates or doors where visitors are authorized to enter into the facility. Personal authentication devices are becoming more and more familiar to a wider audience these days. If a gate is unmanned, a card reader system should be installed for authorizing passage of each person. Also, the gate itself would have to be designed so that it cannot be easily bypassed. Furthermore, bulk-type X-ray devices and/or trace-type devices may be deployed for detecting dangerous objects.

One important feature in an access/egress control systems is the ability to track at all times where the persons are inside the facility AFTER having been granted access. This function is essential for preventing double usage of ID cards.

Standoff distance

The perimeter acts as the first line of the physical security system. It is expected for providing protection against basic low-level threats. The site sits between the perimeter and the buildings. As an open space the site should provide a unique opportunity for early identification of unauthorized intrusion.

NOTE: In fact you may use the site open space to calculate the standoff distance between the outside perimeter (which is often designated as the public areas) to the critical facilities or buildings inside the perimeter (which are the restricted access area).

- *A standoff is the distance between an asset and a threat.*

For protection of highly sensitive assets against highly targeted threats, you may find it necessary to extend the dimensions of perimeter beyond the standard limits. This is especially necessary when there are threats associated with the use of explosive devices.

Space protection devices are detectors capable of registering the presence of individuals in the protected open space area. You may use them to monitor the status of the site open space.

A blast from a bomb can make the whole building collapse. Such collapse would be a function of the magnitude of the blast, which could only be effectively mitigated through increasing the stand-off distance.

NOTE: Generally there are two categories of explosives, which are high brisance explosives and low brisance explosives. They typically fall into three types of configurations, which are solid, liquid and gas. Charge Weight is the factor that establishes the densities of the explosive types as well as the subsequent encasement materials and design parameters of the devices complete with the firing trains. The avoidance criteria would aid in establishing deterrent and deployment difficulties for the explosive devices.

Perimeter items

There are many perimeter items that deserve your attention. Below shows some examples. For in-depth study of these items and others refer to the chapter on Technologies and Equipment Applications.

Examples of items for deployment in the Site Perimeter may include:

● Perimeter Fence

● Landscaping

● Vehicle Barriers

● Secured Gate

● Signage

Examples of items for deployment in the Inner Perimeter may include:

● Site Lighting

● CCTV

● Standoff Distance

Examples of items for deployment in the Building may include:

- Access/egress control devices

- Door Alarms

- CCTV

NOTE: An access/egress control device can be a card reader, a PIN pad, a biometric device or any other kind of identification device capable of using characteristic of a person or the properties of the credential the person possesses for identifying the person.

On the other hand, security consideration for buildings and structures should be placed on external features such as doors, windows, walls, materials, and skylights.

NOTE: Physical condition of the perimeter material must be regularly inspected and maintained.

Explosive events

An explosion can rapidly release energy in the form of light, heat, sound, and shock wave. A shock wave has highly compressed air spreading out radically outward, often at supersonic velocities. However, as the shock wave expands the pressures will decrease rapidly. The duration of an explosive event is usually as short as in thousandths of a second.

Direct air-blast effects refer to the damage caused by the high-intensity pressures of the air-blast. It is the primary damage mechanism of an explosion. The intensity of the blast pressures is the function of the charge weight together with the standoff distance to the protected space.

Diffraction effects can be caused by corners of a building, which may confine the air-blast and prolong its duration. Also, late in the explosion process the shock wave will become negative and will eventually create suction. In other words, behind the shock wave a vacuum will be created together with strong drag pressure on the building surfaces. Generally speaking, the severity of damage in an explosive event can hardly be predicted with high certainty. This is especially true when structural damage is taking place, that progressive collapse is occurring. Progressive collapse can take place when an initiating localized failure is causing the adjoining members to be overloaded and fail.

Concerning the levels of protection required, you must first estimate the amount of explosive and the resulting blast as these factors are necessary for dictating the level of protection required for preventing a building from collapsing. In other words, the size of the explosive threat must be determined through a comprehensive threat and vulnerability assessment and risk analysis. Generally speaking, the extent of a threat can be determined basing on history and expectation as well as the size of the means of explosive delivery.

Prioritizing improvement

When designing physical security for a new facility (or for a facility retrofit), improvements can be prioritized from the outside perimeter to critical assets (that is, from the outside to the inside). You just have to remember, perimeter protection is the first line of defense in providing physical security so you should act on them first. The second line of defense would be the various interior controls and you should act on them next.

NOTE: When physical perimeter security is needed, it should be located within and integrated into the design of the yard area of the building (lawn area, landscape area …etc) if available. If there is no building yard, it may be necessary to place physical perimeter security measures in public space. This is usually not recommended, but if found necessary (i.e. you have no choice) then it should be done in an unobtrusive manner.

Placement of security barriers should incorporate best design practices and be arranged to comply with standards and regulations such as the American Disabilities Act (ADA) and the Architectural

> Barriers Act (ABA) while providing visual clues to signify important circulation routes and site/building features.

Other concerns

In any case, the location of perimeter security barriers should minimize interruption of traffic circulation, and if possible they should be made compatible with placement of security barriers for other buildings next to yours. You do not really want to stand out from the crowd.

Physical hardening of the targets

Murray Neal (1996) classified physical threats into three major categories, which are Forced Entry Threats, Ballistic Threats, and Explosive Blast Threats. He recommended an approach to physical security which focuses on the Physical "Hardening" or "Armoring" of the target (for example, say, the use of physical hardening doors and window assemblies) instead of over reliance on ancillary devices. As he asserted, "anything that is electrical, mechanical or biological can and will have problems and failures". He further believed that the physical hardening approach can reduce the redundancy required for electronic devices due to their limitations and restraints placed upon them.

Situational crime prevention (NEW TOPIC)

This is a pretty important component of police activity at the local level. Also known as target hardening, different methods are used to improve prospects of identifying and deterring crimes. In other words, you aim at reducing the criminal opportunities which arise from the routines of everyday life. The implementation and effectiveness of CCTV have been the focuses.

Reducing the rewards of crime is also an attractive technique set of situational prevention. The focus is on removing items or situations that would be conducive to crimes being committed.

Environmental Conditions and Design

CPTED (NEW TOPIC)

Opportunity is the crime component most readily influenced by security measures. Crime Prevention Through Environmental Design (CPTED) strategies aim at deterring crime through reducing the opportunity to commit crimes. Practically speaking, they may be considered within the following categories:

- Access control, for example, the physical guidance of vehicles and people going to and coming from a space through judicious placement of entrances, exits, landscaping, lighting, and control devices …etc.

- Territorial reinforcement, which refers to the use of physical attributes that express ownership, reinforce territoriality, and designates a gradient from public to restricted spaces.

- Surveillance refers to the placement of physical features, activities and people in order to maximize visibility by others during their normal activities.

- Image and maintenance, which indicates that the space is being used and regularly attended to. Keep in mind, well used areas are usually less susceptible to crime.

> NOTE: The goal of deterrence is the creation of an environment which is highly unattractive to criminals.

The concept of Defensible Space

In order to provide maximum control, an environment should first be divided into smaller, clearly defined areas or zones, which serve as the focal points for security protection. A defensible space is an area that has been made as a zone of protection by the design characteristics that create it.

Under the defensible space concept, all areas should be marked as either public, semi-private or private. The designation serves to define the acceptable use of each zone as well as to determine who has a right to occupy it.

Public Zones are generally open to anyone and are the least secure of all the zones. Building grounds, public parking lots and lobby areas are examples of this kind of zone. Semi-private Zones are areas created as a buffer between public and private zones. Examples include office waiting areas, meeting rooms and the like. They have design features for establishing definite and clear transitional boundaries between the zones. Private Zones are areas of restricted entry with access being controlled and limited to specific individuals or groups.

NOTE: A clearzone is an area surrounding the perimeter of a facility. It is made free of shrubs and trees. It has well-maintained landscaping that provides no hiding places for an adversary. It serves as a demarcation zone that makes unauthorized entry way more noticeable. You should NOT allow materials or objects of any sort to be stored over there to obstruct view.

NOTE: Parking space must be properly planned. Executive parking section should be separated from the Employee parking section, with spaces numbered and assigned. Employee parking needs not have assigned spaces but sufficient spaces must be made available. Visitor parking should be located close to the main entrance, while delivery parking should be located close to the dock that is under constant security observation.

Enhanced lighting in the parking lot would be recommended if there are concerns about violence in the neighborhood area.

Controlled Area, Restricted Area, Strong Room and Vault

A controlled area is a room, office or building to which access has to be monitored, limited, and controlled. Admittance to a controlled area should be limited to those who have officially authorized business within the area. Examples of these areas include:

- an area where classified / sensitive information is handled, processed, or stored.

- an area that houses equipment that is significantly valuable or critical to the business operations.

- an area where uncontrolled access can interfere with or disrupt personnel assigned to the area.

- an area where equipment or operations can constitute a potential safety hazard.

A restricted area, in contrast, is a room, office or building to which access has to be strictly controlled. Admittance to such area should be limited to personnel assigned to the area or persons who have been specifically authorized access to the area. Visitors and uncleared personnel who want in must be escorted.

A strongroom is an enclosed space typically constructed of solid building materials. It is normally used for the storage for classified material such as firearms. Protection of strong room is normally supplemented by human guards and/or alarm systems.

A vault is a completely enclosed space with a high degree of protection against forced entry. It is typically constructed to meet rigid specifications. The wall, floor, and ceiling construction are all in accordance with nationally recognized standards of construction practice.

Attractive nuisance

You want to be extremely careful on this. Under the attractive nuisance doctrine (which is part of the law of torts), a facility owner can be held liable for injuries to children trespassing on the facility if the injury is caused by a hazardous object or condition inside the facility that is likely to attract children who are unable to appreciate the risk involved. It can be applied to virtually anything inside the facility.

FYI: Security Design for VA Facility

<u>Before proceeding to the next section, you want to take a look at the VA design guidelines for life-safety protected VA facility (for your reference only – VA design is not an exam requirement)</u>:

The physical security of facilities should require the use of concentric levels of control and protection to provide progressively enhanced levels of security. According to this design, the first point of control should be at the perimeter of the property consisting of fences and other barriers with one or two points of entry through gates controlled by security personnel. The second point of control should be at the building perimeter consisting of doors and other openings protected as appropriate to the level of protection needed with or without the first point of control. The third point of control should be to segregate with barriers and hardware generally accessible areas from staff-only areas. The fourth point of control should be to segregate authorized from unauthorized staff areas with barriers and access controls such as card reader-activated hardware. The fifth point of control should be to restrict access to restricted areas to a minimum with card-reader access controls, CCTV monitors, intrusion detection alarms, and forced-entry-resistant construction.

Regarding STAND-OFF DISTANCE, they do not allow vehicle to be parked or be permitted to travel closer than 25 feet to any protected facility. Regarding perimeter fences, they should consist of fences, walls, a combination of both, and gates as needed for access. They should have sufficient lateral support to resist overturning by manual force and should be on or in close proximity to the perimeter of the property. Additionally, they should have at least 6 feet (1.8 m) between potential horizontal footholds or designed with other anti-climb measures.

For life-safety protected facility, they require fences made of metal and of heavy industrial-grade construction with bar spacing at a maximum of 5 inches on center. They do not recommend the use of chain link fences and gates. Regarding gates, pedestrian and bicycle gates should swing in the outward direction and at the same time be made fully accessible to persons with disabilities. Vehicular security gates should be sliding or cantilevered with no tracks and only wide enough to accommodate one vehicle lane.

Regarding facility entrance, keep in mind public access to the facility should always be restricted to a single or limited number of entrances. Screening vestibule if implemented should have sufficient space and be provided with power, telecommunications, and data connections for installation of access control and screening equipment that may be used should the need arise. Always prevent access from drop-off to lobby in a straight line of travel. Always provide sufficient size to accommodate several people with mobility aids.

On the other hand, at all public entrances you should provide the required connections for temporary installation of metal detectors and package screening equipment and sufficient space for their installation without restricting emergency egress. You should locate screening equipment in a manner that will prevent passage into the building or facility without passing through the devices. If screening devices are not permanently installed, always provide secure storage in close proximity to their installation location.

Regarding vehicle entrance, it is recommended that access roads for all vehicles be allowed for separate driveways to the building entrance, service yard, or parking. Access roads from entrances to parking for each vehicle type should be separated, but may be connected for maintenance and emergency vehicles through gates controlled by access cards. Additionally, access roads should be configured to prevent vehicles from attaining speeds in excess of 25 mph.

Regarding site lighting, the desired illumination and enhancement of trees, landscaping, and buildings should be provided without providing dark shadowy areas compromising safety and security. Site lighting should provide CCTV and other surveillance support with illumination levels and color that assists in proper identification. Illumination levels should be in compliance with the Illumination Engineering Society of North America (IESNA), VA Design Guides, and local and state governing agencies. Signage and way finding should be enhanced by site lighting, including providing improved security by assisting pedestrians and vehicles to locate their destinations expeditiously.

CCTV

The use of CCTV systems has the purpose of deterring crime and facilitating the apprehension and conviction of people involved in criminal activity. You need to do your best in increasing the likelihood that the images recovered from your CCTV systems are sufficient enough to enable law enforcement officials to identify the people of interest depicted therein. In order to accurately identify a person, specific individual features of the person such as the detailed shape of the eyes, ears, nose, mouth, and chin must be clearly distinguished. Identification is facilitated if the ability to distinguish smaller facial features and the ability to derive measurements of these features is possible.

A proper and complete camera system should include one or more cameras, a monitor for viewing the camera images, a recording device for capturing selected images, as well as software and/or a switching system for controlling the method of selecting and storing images.

Camera

- When selecting the cameras to use, consideration should be given to any need for recording audio with the video from one or more cameras. You should also seek advice on any possible legal problems that are unique to audio recording.

- The number and placement of cameras must be sufficient to provide adequate coverage and detail in the monitored area. You should have cameras placed where they can record images with no obstruction. If a window or glass is present, you must properly position the camera to minimize reflection and glare.

- Exterior cameras that are intended to record images of vehicles must be placed in such a way capable of providing direct views of the vehicle so that the license plate can be made clearly visible.

- There should be at least one camera for every exit, and the exit cameras should be aimed toward the interior rather than the exterior of your facility.

- For serious security effort, wireless camera should be highly discouraged!!! Performance is way too unstable to be acceptable.

Stationary dome cameras are mounted on wall or ceiling and are mostly used indoors or outdoors. Most of them are vandal resistant. Speed dome cameras are typically high-resolution and can rotate 360°, thus making them the ideal choices for video surveillance of large rooms. IP/network cameras allow output to be streamed over a LAN, WAN, or the Internet for viewing and recording.

 NOTE: Resolution and sensitivity are the key factors to consider when selecting cameras for any CCTV installation. Resolution deals with the sharpness of a displayed image and is typically noted as lines on a screen. On the other hand, sensitivity of a camera to light is measured in lux. Generally speaking, a lower-lux camera is more sensitive in low light levels than a high-lux camera. For lowlight applications, you want to deploy cameras with infrared LEDs. Intensifier technology can allow for the camera to see in low-light environments without IR LEDs. It works by amplifying existing light.

Monitor

- A monitor capable of operating in an under-scan mode is recommended as it permits the viewer to observe the entire field-of-view that is being recorded.

Recorder

- Video-camera systems may use an analog based videocassette recorder (VCR) or a digital video recorder (DVR), or even a PC-based digital recording capture station. Analog VCRs should be configured to record each image at a minimum line resolution of 240 visible lines. Disk based DVR should be configured to record each frame at a minimum resolution of 640 x 480 pixels. If video compression is desired, use lossless compression. If lossy compression is the only option, be sure to have an alarm-mode available such that the highest possible image quality can be rendered upon a security event. This type of recorder must also be equipped with a buffer capable of retaining the several minutes of data prior to the alarm trigger.

- For tape, the quality of image reproduction can reduce overtime. Also, if you run a 3-hr tape at a 12-hr setting as an example, less video frames are recorded.

- If tape based VCR is preferred, to save tape space you should consider to use time-lapse recorders that are capable of recording video at rates lower than 60 images per second. Videotapes should be retained for a minimum of one month prior to being reused.

- Some systems include triggers that allow for the recording of images at a rate, or in a sequence, that differs from the normal operating mode. If you are to use this type of systems, be sure to test recording thoroughly.

 NOTE: Digital video recorder (DVR) is rapidly replacing the traditional VCR recording device. Video images are typically saved onto the hard drive, which can eliminate the need for tape storage entirely. Some models offer the ability to offload video clips to a CD or even thumb drive. Some newer DVRs are even Internet-ready, meaning the user can view live, record, and playback functions from anywhere.

Video Cables

Coaxial cables (such as RG 59, with BNC connectors) are mostly used for the traditional video capturing system, although UTP cable may be required for IP based cameras.

Switch

- With a sequential switch the video signals from each camera are switched in sequence. Dwell time for each input is usually adjustable.
- Sequential switching is simple to implement, but the viewer can only view one output at a time. One way to work around is to setup alarms from the relevant areas.
- Screen splitters allow you to view all outputs simultaneously. However, the sizes of viewable pictures get way smaller on screen.
- Video multiplexers allow multiple streams of video signal to be transmitted to a single viewer or recorder simultaneously.

Other guidelines

Below are some additional guidelines for CCTV implementation:

- Poor lighting degrades the quality of video images. So, don't forget to ensure there is adequate and balanced lighting in the monitored area. Some cameras have light intensifiers built-in to aid in low-light operation.

- High pressure sodium lights and/or metal halides are good sources of lighting.

- Infrared lighting may be used to provide improved low light performance for monochrome cameras. However, infrared lighting is never supported by standard color cameras as they tend to filter out the infrared spectrum.

- Cameras may need proper coverings and environmental controls for shielding them from tampering. Do remember, clear coverings that are placed in front of camera lenses could in fact reduce image quality.

- You may use PTZ (Pan Tilt Zoom) units to pivot the cameras.

- Possible sources of noise include poor circuit design, heat, over-amplification, external influences, automatic gain control, and transmission systems. It is recommended that you have your CCTV systems placed on isolated circuits that are properly grounded for reducing interference and signal degradation. Line loss between each camera and the recorder should not cause the signal to fall below 45dB.

- Time, date, and camera information are highly useful pieces of information in investigations and must be properly preserved. Test recordings should be conducted to ensure that this requirement is being properly met.

- Recordings that depict criminal activity have to be preserved with a documented chain of custody.

- You should establish a program of regular CCTV system maintenance. Adequate system documentation must be included on site. Point-of-contact information for system installer and/or system maintenance organization must be made ready for reference. An in-depth site plan showing all equipment placement is a MUST.

- You should specify documented procedures for ensuring that your employees know what to do during a criminal incident.

- Video motion detector (VMD) works by comparing grey scale levels on the images frame by frame. The problem is that variations are often the results of environmental issues (snow, rain, lights…etc), thus producing quite many false alarms.

NOTE: Night lighting could affect the performance of CCTV so there is a direct relationship between the CCTV system and the lighting systems.

NOTE: If the CCTV signals are recorded, you must ensure there are proper procedures in place to address the following issues: How will tapes (or other media) be indexed and cataloged for easy retrieval? Will the tapes (or other media) be stored on site or off site? Who will have access to them? What is the procedure required for accessing them? And how long will they be kept before being destroyed?

Building Openings

Openings in buildings may be divided into four major categories, which are doors, windows, ventilation and utility openings.

Doors

An intruder will most likely select a door that looks easiest to break in. Doors that are considered as "easy to break in" typically include:

- Fragile doors that can simply be "kicked in".

- Door locks that can be picked, be hammered off, be pried off, or be drilled out.

- Doors that can be pried open, or door with frames that can be spread apart with a spreader bar.

- Doors with panes of glass in or beside doors that can be broken so the intruder can easily reach in and unlock the lock.

Generally speaking, a door that opens into the protected space is more secure than one that opens out. On the other hand, a secured door that cannot be opened for egress could be a safety threat to the building occupants.

Secure door design

A door designed for one person to pass at a time is called a personal man door. A typical one has hinges on one side and a latch on the other. Generally speaking, the heavier the door the more secure it is. A higher rated fire door would be more secure than a door without fire rating. Hollow core doors are weak and should not be used.

Generally speaking, the strike plate's attachment to the doorframe is considered as the weakest point in the entire door/doorframe/lock system. You want to ensure only high security strike plates are used. These special plates come with a heavy gauge metal reinforcing plate which mounts under the cosmetic strike plate. Long screws are used for securing the strike to the wall framing.

Strike plate

Generally speaking, the strike plate's attachment to the doorframe is considered as the weakest point in the entire door/doorframe/lock system. You want to ensure only high security strike plates are used. These special plates come with a heavy gauge metal reinforcing plate which mounts under the cosmetic strike plate. Long screws are used for securing the strike to the wall framing.

Door hinge

Door hinge with non-removable pins - On this kind of hinges, the pins are all held in place by a setscrew in such a way that when the door is closed, the setscrew will not be accessible.

Door hinge with safety studs - This kind of hinges would come in full mortised type only. The hinge would sit in routed-out insets in the door and frame. The studs would extend from one hinge leaf and a hole would be punched in the corresponding position on the opposite leaf. Therefore, when the door is closed, the stud would sit in the hole.

Door hinge with crimped pins - This kind of hinges is designed in such a way that the hinge pin would not be removable. The hinge pin is intentionally made longer than the hinge height, inserted into the hinge, and spun on the end for creating a rivet-type end on the top and bottom of the pin.

Door window

Doors with windows can be protected by having bars on the window opening. A door with a window high up on the door would make it difficult for one to reach through to the latch, which would be good from a security standpoint.

Forced entry

Regarding forced entry, you want to know the types of attack implementations that are possible so you may plan your door design accordingly. Blunt impacting implements involve using tools such as two handed sledge hammers, one handed hammers, clubs, bars, bricks ...etc. Sharp impacting implements often involve the use of axe, pointed devices, ripping bars, pipes or other objects with sharp edge. Chemical deterioration involves using chemicals that are highly caustic and corrosive. Thermal stressing involves the weakening of the protective armor using chemicals that can be ignited to burn through or weaken an area. Assisted Attack may involve utilizing either ballistic or explosive blast attacks.

Windows

Window units may be fixed, operable, or a mixture of both. Commonly used window frame materials are aluminum, steel and wood. Fixed windows can offer better air infiltration and water penetration resistance, and will generally require less maintenance. Operable window may be classified as sliding seal windows and compression seal windows. Compression seal windows can provide better long-term air infiltration and water penetration resistance than sliding seal windows as there is less friction and wear on the weather stripping. One important design consideration for operable windows is the resistance to wind loads when they are in the open position.

Window openings can be the weak point where an intruder can break the glass and enter into the building. Security-wise, a facility with small windows is better than a facility with large windows. Windows high up on the structure that are difficult to reach from the outside are always more preferable.

Ventilation and utility openings

Openings for heating, ventilation and air conditioning may be used by an intruder for penetrating into the building. These openings should be covered with grills or louvers. Air handler intakes should be located on the roofs or high up on the side of the facility. If the existing air intakes are easily accessible, elevate them above ground level by, say, extending the duct.

Utility openings, hatches (for roof access and skylights...etc) and manholes (eg. electric power manholes, telecommunications wiring conduits or chases, plumbing, piping and drainage...etc) are not designed for passage, even though they can be passed by intruders. You may want to install grilles or bars around them.

> NOTE: Practically speaking, all vents and ducts (with both dimensions over, say, six inches) that penetrate the facility's perimeter should be alarmed. Also, Windows less than, say, 18 feet from the ground level, or otherwise accessible through other means (roof, trees ...etc) should also be alarmed.

Electrical locks

Installing electrically powering door hardware requires an understanding of what amount and direction of electrical flow is required. This can become a highly complicated matter with multiple systems because different devices may use power at different levels.

A simple electromagnetic lock uses a magnet that takes electric power to hold the door closed. Magnetic locks are generally available in different strengths (from 300 pounds to 3000 pounds for breaking the lock). It is quite secure as long as power is applied correctly. Usually, power is 12V DC (direct current) or 24V DC.

Do keep in mind, there must be a way to cancel the power when people inside need to exit during emergency. This may be done via an extra switch installed on the wall inside the door. You also need to figure out a way to keep the lock working when the power fails. Backup power would be required to achieve this.

Electric keypad is different from a mechanical lock in that power is required. Sometimes it can be provided with a battery such that no hard wiring is required. Generally speaking, alkaline based batteries are good enough for several thousand cycles before replacement is necessary. The weakest point security-wise is the key combination - once the combination is made known by the user, anyone who knows it can unlock it.

Another way of controlling a door is through an intercom system. You need a receptionist standby to respond to the intercom request. Intercoms may be wired similar to all other electrical devices, just that special attention may be necessary for shielding the devices from weather.

> NOTE: Power must be properly planned for these devices. You may rely on a single line diagram (aka single line power distribution diagram) to do the planning. This diagram has a set of drawings which shows at a glance how power supply is distributed through the building facility.
>
> An emergency power supply may be implemented through providing an emergency generator to generate electricity when the main power supply fails (through an Automatic Transfer Switch). The generator is basically a device with a diesel or gasoline engine hooked to it.

Gates and Fencing

ChainLink Fencing

Baselevel fence guideline calls for galvanized steel chainlink fence post with a 6 ft minimum fabric height. Enhanced level fence guideline calls for galvanized steel chainlink fence post with an 8-ft minimum fabric height. Fence fabric should be of a one-piece form and should be coated with zinc or polyvinyl chloride (PVC).

 NOTE: You should consider using PVC over zinccoated steel for application in highly corrosive environment.

Baselevel fabric wire gauge should be a minimum standard wire gauge of No. 9 and mesh pattern of max 2 inch diamond mesh. Enhanced level chainlink would use No. 6 or No. 8 gauge fencing fabric instead. Average dimension between line posts should be no more than 10 ft center-to-center between posts and parallel to the fence grade. Post hole depth should be a minimum of 24 inches plus additional 3 inches for each single foot increase in fence height over 4 ft.

Chainlink Gates

Entry gates with perimeter fence double swing gates should come with a maximum 2.5inch clearance between the bottom rail and the finished grade. They should have reinforced steel latch with hardened steel padlock protection.

AntiClimb/AntiCut Fencing

Specialized anticlimb / anticut fence in the form of wirepanel mesh fencing should be considered. Wirepanel mesh fabric wire gauge should be of No. 8 wire gauge as a minimum. Wirepanel mesh pattern should be made nonclimbable with 0.5 inch by 3 inch properly welded at each intersection.

Aesthetically pleasing fence

Ornamental Fencing would be used if site conditions and local codes call for the use of aesthetically pleasing fence materials.

Fence topping

The kinds of fence topping may include barbedwire topping or concertina barbedwire tape topping or a combination of both. Generally, for base level barbedwire topping guideline you would attach a threestrand of barbed wire to a 2-ft high single outrigger. For enhanced level climb resistance you would use double Y style outriggers with 3 strand barbed wire. On the other hand, for concertinawire topping you would attach 12 gauge stainless steel wires to 2 ft high double Y style outriggers.

Fence maintenance

Periodic treatment of the perimeter line should be conducted to prevent vegetation growth. You may want to provide a 1-ft wide vegetation-free zone with fencing placed in center of the zone. Stretching of the fence fabric may allow an adversary to move under the fence. It may therefore be appropriate to anchor the bottom fabric of the fence to create delay. Tunneling under fences may be effectively prevented via a continuous concrete curb at the base of fence.

Electronic Gate Opening

Electrical gate operators should be Underwriters Laboratory (UL) listed. You would need heavy duty, high frequency electrical models that are designed to open and close sliding or other types of gates. There should be a maximum 2.5 inch clearance between the bottom tension bar and the finished grade. Properly sized electrical motors should be selected basing on factors such as gate weight, duty rating, and frequency of operation. The generally recommended minimum gate travel speed is 1 ft per second, with speed adjusting capability preferred. There should be positive limit switches in place for sensing the position of the gate and provide proper control to prevent damage to the gate operator. Manual operation feature is a must in the case of power failure.

Fence signage

You should post "No Trespassing" signs at 50 ft intervals, in multiple languages to be consistent with the local population. You may also want to include the appropriate federal, state and local laws which prohibit trespassing.

Entrance signage

It is generally recommended that at the primary entrance you post the address of the site so that first responder can easily confirm the address location.

Fence mounted sensors

Fence mounted sensors can detect vibrations on fence fabric that are associated with sawing, cutting, climbing, or lifting. They are typically not too reliable in areas where high vibrations are likely to be encountered, especially when in close proximity to roadway activity. They would perform best when mounted directly to the fence fabric, with each sensor connected in series along the fence with a common cable for forming a single zone of protection.

Locking device

Locks may be broadly classified into three general classes, which are those that operate on purely mechanical principles; those that combine electrical energy with mechanical operations; and those that are highly electronic - they add to electro-mechanical lock devices various logic operations associated with integrated circuits (ICs).

Mechanical locks

Key locks are the most common mechanical locks. They are used primarily for delaying, discouraging, or deterring theft and unauthorized access. Warded Lock is a very simple "legacy" device exemplified by the open, see-through keyway and the long, barrel-like key. Lever Lock is inherently susceptible to picking and is mostly used for desk, cabinet, and locker installations. Pin Tumbler Lock is most popular for use with exterior and interior building doors. You want one with at least 6 pins (a 6-pin configuration would be considered as a high-security lock.

Combination lock is manipulation-resistant which can provide a high degree of protection. It is often used for safeguarding classified or sensitive material. Note that when a security container or vault door is used to safeguard classified information, it should be equipped with a changeable 3-position, dial-type combination lock.

Combination padlock is designed primarily for attachment to a mounted hasp. It is not rated for resistance to physical attack, and should be used either as a removable padlock in conjunction with bar-lock cabinets and other conventional hasp-type locks, or by fastening the security cover of the padlock to the surface of a container. It may also be used on desks, storage cabinets, filing cabinets, sliding door cabinets, and virtually any type of container through the use of an eyelet or loop that can fit the tolerances of the opening of the padlock.

Electro-Mechanical Locks

Electro-mechanical locks are mostly used for controlling entry into an area. Instead of using a key, they may be opened through pushing a series of numeric buttons. They may be either electrically or mechanically activated. Do note that they should be used for access control in conjunction with other mechanisms since they do not really provide a high degree of security when used alone.

Security Strength of the Door Locks

You will be surprised to find that most building codes in fact do not require a lock on exterior doors! Anyway, there is a grading system for measuring the security and durability of door locks. The American National Standards Institute (ANSI) has standards that were developed and maintained by The Builders Hardware Manufacturers Association Inc (BHMA). These standards serve to measure the security and durability performance of door locks.

There are other security features that deserve your consideration:

- Anti-Drill Feature is usually implemented by installing hardened steel chips within the lock housing of the door lock. When a drill bit hits these steel chips, it will get torn up.

- There are saw-resistant bolts available - they usually come with internal anti-saw pins to make sawing difficult.

- Double cylinder deadbolt locks have keyholes on both sides of the door. While this is good security-wise, it may create a fire safety danger to people inside the room.

UL Testing for locks and locking devices

The Underwriters Laboratories is a not-for-profit independent testing organization. Its sole purpose and function is to test for public safety and crime prevention. There are a number of UL tests and standards that may be of relevance in the context of physical security. Below shows some examples:

Burglary Classification TL-15 deals with combination-locked safe designed to offer a limited degree of protection against attack by common mechanical and electrical hand tools and any combination of these means. The requirement is to successfully resist entry for a net working time of 15 minutes when attacked with common hand tools, picking tools, mechanical or portable electric tools, grinding points, carbide drills and pressure applying devices or mechanisms.

Burglary Classification TL-30 signifies a combination-locked safe designed to offer a moderate degree of protection against attack by common mechanical and electrical hand tools and any combination of these means. The requirement is to successfully resist entry for a net working time of 30 minutes when attacked with common hand tools, picking tools, mechanical or portable electric tools, grinding points, carbide drills and pressure applying devices or mechanisms, abrasive cutting wheels and power saws.

The UL140 Relocking Device Standard deals with relocking devices that are intended to relock the bolt mechanism or door of a vault, safe, or chest in the event that the combination lock is subjected to attack. Relocking devices for the following are covered: Light vault doors, Heavy vault doors, and Safes or chests.

The UL768 Standard for Safety for Combination Locks covers combination locks intended for attachment on doors of safes, chests, vaults, and the like, to provide a means of locking the boltwork against unauthorized opening. It tests the ability of combination locks to resist unauthorized opening of the combination locks by sense of sight, touch, or hearing.

Lighting

In the security design you cannot afford to ignore the element of lighting. Lighting is often a relevant issue in security related matter and is seen as necessary for providing a safe environment. In general, all gates and doors must have proper night lighting. Vehicle entry points need maximum lighting. Additionally, there should be one strong light on every corner of a building. Areas visible to the street should be well illuminated.

Flood light can flood a particular area with light. Streetlight can illuminate the immediate area. Fresnel light is for glare project application. Searchlight is good as supplementary lighting.

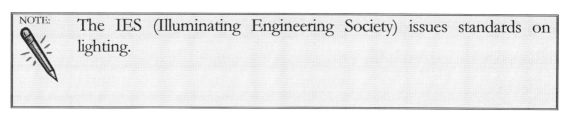

NOTE: The IES (Illuminating Engineering Society) issues standards on lighting.

Masonry walls

Masonry has been used in building construction for thousands of years. It can be used to form a durable cladding system and to achieve various aesthetic effects. In addition to forming exterior cladding, masonry walls can serve as a portion of the structural framing for the building. Masonry walls can also be deployed to increase the fire resistance of the wall system or structural elements.

Masonry walls can be single or multi-wythe. A wythe of masonry describes the thickness of wall equal to the thickness of the individual units. Structural masonry walls are typically constructed using concrete masonry. The concrete masonry can be reinforced both vertically and horizontally to achieve the required flexural resistance. If structural masonry walls are to serve as the exterior walls, a second wythe of masonry is usually recommended.

NOTE: Double Wythe Walls should be chosen as standard for all finished buildings and interior administrative space. Corner Guards of stainless steel should be used for protection of masonry at the service entries and at other locations that are subject to impact.

You may consider the use of masonry walls to compartmentalize your facility. When under bombing or fire, masonry walls can do well for containment of fires. They can also be used to structurally stabilize as well as defer much of the weight load produced by a blast. Walls made using 8-inch solid or solidly grouted concrete masonry units as well as those made of 12-inch hollow concrete masonry units with sand-filled cores can deter bullets from high-powered firearms without problems.

 NOTE: Within a building there are often areas that need to be more protective than the others. This may be accomplished by strengthening the walls, floor, and ceiling. This may also be done through eliminating glass based structures (windows and the like).

Intrusion Detection System and Devices

Intrusion detection systems should cover the entire length of the perimeter of a detection area, and should be equipped with a redundant power source for a period of not less than four hours. Perimeter intrusion detection should provide average false alarm rates of no more than one false alarm per week per sensor. On the other hand, interior intrusion detection should provide false alarm rates of no more than one false alarm every three months per sensor. Detection probability should be at a 95 percent confidence level.

Control Panel

The control panel is the heart of the Intruder Alarm system. All the parts of the Intruder Alarm are linked to this panel, which is connected to the mains electricity and has a battery fitted inside to run the system in case of power failure.

RKP, Sounders and Panic button

A Remote Keypad (RKP) can also be used to control the Intruder Alarm system. This is usually fitted somewhere near the exit point for switching the system on and off.

An outside sounder is usually fitted at high level for making a lot of noise. It usually comes with anti-tamper protection and a separate battery. A Strobe light is also available for flashing when the sounder activates. An internal sounder, on the other hand, is fitted somewhere inside the protected area for indicating fault conditions as well as full alarm activations.

A Personal Attack button (aka 'panic' button) is a small unit that has one or two recessed red buttons. When pressed the unit would cause the alarm to activate immediately.

Exterior sensors

Exterior sensors may be classified as passive or active, covert or visible, line of sight or terrain-following, volumetric or line detection, and application (such as buried-line, fence associated, or freestanding).

- Visible sensors are in plain view of the intruder and may deter the intruder from acting.

- Terrain-following sensors can detect accurately on flat and irregular terrain.

- Passive sensors can detect energy emitted by the target of interest or detect the change of the surrounding natural field caused by the target.

- Buried line sensor is in the form of a line buried in the ground.

- Pressure or seismic sensors are those passive, covert, terrain-following sensors that are buried and are supposed to respond to disturbances of the soil caused by an intruder.

- Magnetic field sensors are passive, covert, terrain following sensors that are buried and are supposed to respond to changes in the local magnetic field caused by the movement of metallic material nearby.

- Fence-associated sensor is either mounted on a fence or forms a sensor fence. Fence disturbance sensor can respond to mechanical disturbances produced on the fence. Coaxial cable sensors can provide the desired portability since maintenance is easier than the fiber disturbance type sensors.

- Freestanding sensor is being mounted on a support in free space.

Infrared sensors

Active infrared sensors transmit infrared signals to a receiver. To work smoothly they require line of sight, that the signal must be projected over a clear path in such a way that the line of sight would remain unblocked.

Microwave sensors

Microwave sensors flood a designated area with an electronic field such that a movement in the area would disturb the field and sets off an alarm. To work properly the detection area should be made free of obstructions and should not be in close proximity to other high frequency signals. If the area is on a grass land the grass should be cut to less than 3 inches. Note that gravel surface prepared for water drainage would be better than a grass surface. Also, metal objects such as dumpsters, shipping crates, trashcans ...etc are dead spots that should be avoided whenever possible.

Bistatic microwave sensors

Bistatic microwave sensors are active, visible, line of sight, freestanding sensors that have at least two identical antennas installed at the opposite ends of a detection zone. One is connected to a transmitter operating at 10 GHz or 24 GHz. The other is connected to a receiver. The sensors would respond to changes in the vector sum caused by objects moving within the viewing field of the receiver. For this to work the ground must be of a flat surface. Bistatic microwave sensors are good in that they can tolerate a wide range of environmental conditions without generating nuisance alarms.

NOTE: Do note that there is a zone of no detection in the first few meters right in front of the antennas (known as the "offset distance).

Dual technology sensors

A typical dual technology sensor may use both microwave and passive infrared (PIR) sensor circuitry. PIR sensors can pick up heat signatures from intruders and perform measurement basing on activation differentials that are typically set at 3 degrees Fahrenheit. An alarm will be triggered when either the microwave or the PIR sensor detects an intruder.

Linear beam sensors

Linear beam sensors transmit a beam of infrared light to a remote receiver (for up to 1,000 feet), effectively creating an electronic fence. When the beam is broken, an alarm signal will be generated. The good thing about this technology is that it has a high probability of detection and a low false alarm rate, due to the fact that infrared beam is not affected by changes in thermal radiation, fluorescent lights, electronic frequency interference (EFI), and/or radio frequency interference (RFI).

Volumetric-protection sensors

Volumetric-protection sensors can detect the presence or actions of an intruder almost anywhere within the entire room. They are typically used for providing highly sensitive and invisible means of detection in high-risk areas. Do note that improper application can result in frequent false alarms.

Glass Break Sensors

Glassbreak sensors provide intrusion detection for windows and doors with glass panes. They can be mounted on the window, window frame, wall, or ceiling easily through mounting adhesive.

There are three basic types of glass break sensors, which are acoustic sensors, shock sensors, and dual technology sensors. You should opt for using dual technology sensors as they can significantly reduce false alarms from background noise.

Metallic-foil window tape can be used for detecting glass breakage. Strips of thin foil may be affixed to a glass surface. Breaking the glass would at the same time fracture the foil, which can interrupt the circuit and trigger the alarm.

Nuisance alarm VS False alarm

A nuisance alarm refers to any alarm that is not caused by an actual intrusion. In a perfect sensor system, the NAR should be zero. However, in the real world, this would be impossible due to all sorts of external factors in the operating environment. Therefore you will need to have an alarm assessment system in place. False alarms are special - they refer to those nuisance alarms that are generated by the equipment itself.

To reduce nuisance alarms, special dual technology device may be considered. A dual technology device can work in such a way that it would not fire an alarm until both sensors are alarmed. The two basic techniques for combining multiple sensors are the OR combinations and the AND combinations. With the OR combination, an alarm would be generated when any of the participating sensors is activated. With the AND combination, a single intrusion attempt that fails to activate two or more sensors simultaneously will NOT trigger an alarm.

NOTE: A preferred method for handling security alarms would require a system operator to assess all the running alarms with the aid of an Information System that is capable of establishing the time order of assessment for multiple simultaneous alarms. The system should be able to tell the order in which the alarms occur in relation to the physical configuration of the sensors, and be able to identify those alarms in the two adjacent sectors.

Door and Hatch Contact Alarm Switches

These switches should be configured to interface with a security monitoring system. Magnetic door contact switches should be installed at all building exterior doors. Exposed exterior locations should use high security balanced magnetic switches. Industrial doors, gates, and rollup doors should be equipped with high security rugged duty, sealed, wide gap magnetic switches.

Card Reader Systems

Card reader systems for security purpose should incorporate capabilities for interfacing with a computer for displaying alarm conditions and allowing programming of the system. A badge station should be used to allow for the creation and programming of ID badges. Local control panels should be made ready for controlling the doors, card reader units, and access cards. The access card should be a standard credit card size passive component constructed with an integral coding technology. Choices for electrical locking means may include electric strike, magnetic lock, or other approved means.

Problems with most magnetic card reader include dirt and other debris fouling the badge. There could also be problems with the magnetism of the cards - the cards' magnetic memory can be easily corrupted or erased simply by having contact with magnets or by getting too close to other magnetic alarm devices. Also, the readers would not work well outdoor as they cannot afford to get wet or dusty.

Magnetic stripe card is the most common type of card. It has a simple magnetic strip of identifying data. When the card is swiped in a reader, the information is read and looked up in a database. This kind of system is not too expensive and is quite convenient to use. However, it is relatively easy to duplicate the cards or to read the information stored on them (as long as the hacker has the equipment).

Barium ferrite card is also being referred to as magnetic spot card. It is similar to the magnetic stripe card but is capable of offering more security without adding significant cost. It has a thin sheet of magnetic material with round spots arranged in a pattern. Rather than scanning or swiping, one may simply have the card touched to the reader.

Weigand card is a variation of the magnetic stripe card technology. It has a series of specially treated wires with a unique magnetic signature embedded. When the card is swiped through the reader, a sensing coil would detect the signature and then convert it to bits. It is a complex card design which is hard to duplicate but is also hard to reprogram.

A bar-code card carries a bar code, which may be read when the card is swiped in the reader. This kind of system is very low-cost, but is also very easy to fool. An ordinary copy machine can duplicate a bar code well enough to fool the reader.

Biometric Devices (NEW TOPIC)

Biometric identification is typically used to verify identity that has first been established by methods such as an ID card or a PIN, even though it is technically possible to use it entirely alone as the authentication method. Do note that there are two types of failures in biometric identification, which are false rejection (failure to recognize a legitimate user) and false acceptance (erroneous recognition). Even though failure rates can be adjusted by changing the threshold for declaring a match, decreasing one failure rate can have the side effect of increasing the other.

When choosing a biometric capability, you need to consider the factors of equipment cost, failure rates, and user acceptance. Some people dislike biometric devices as they are being perceived as highly intrusive and even dangerous.

Duress systems (NEW TOPIC)

A typical duress system can be wireless, monitored via central station or phone-line dialing, through onsite paging (via SMS or pager), or by onsite security personnel. It can provide these broad functions:

- Sending message through duress alert transmitter (carried by the user)

- Receiving message via a portable receiver or a central message centre

- Acting on the message

An example is the duress system used in a correctional facility. Such a system aims to alert the authorities in a fast and effective manner that there is a security incident that may be threatening the safety of personnel, of other inmates and perhaps even visitors.

Identity management system (NEW TOPIC)

An identity management system can be used to support the management of identities. Through it, you can:

- establish and reestablish an identity

- link a name with the subject or object

- describe an identity

- follow, track and record identity activity

- analyze behavior patterns of identity

- destroy an identity

Functionalities provided by identity management system typically include password management and the provisioning/de-provisioning of identities from resources

Control Unit

All modern alarm systems would have to incorporate a control unit, which may or may not be a separate component. The control unit is for regulating the entire system, turning an alarm system on and off, and transmitting the alarm signal to an annunciator. The method for controlling the alarm system would usually be a key or a digital keypad housed inside the premises to avoid being tampered with. The alarm system would be delayed briefly to allow the user to have sufficient time in gaining access to the system without initiating an alarm too early.

With local systems, the user would have to be responsible for turning the alarm on and off. The local alarm system has circuits within the secured areas that are directly connected to audio or visual signal-producing devices, while the signaling devices are normally mounted on the exterior of the building.

A central-station alarm system is connected to an alarm panel located in a central station such as a local police station or a commercial guard service. When an alarm is triggered, the monitoring station would initiate a response by either calling personnel designated for the area or by dispatching guards accordingly.

A proprietary alarm system is similar to the central station type, except that the alarm panel is located in a manned guardroom that is within the protected premises. The guard force would monitor the system and respond to all alarms. An annunciator is a device that sounds an alarm by visible or audible signals. It should be installed in a way capable of indicating the location of the protected item or premises.

All alarm control units must be physically located within the secured perimeter of the area which the alarms are protecting. They must all be equipped with tamper switches. Also, a minimum of, say, four hours standby power should be made available for all alarm systems, except when a system has been connected to a local uninterrupted emergency power source.

Control Room

A control room should be equipped with television monitors for confirming those images sent from the surveillance cameras. Each personnel in the control room should be assigned to monitor at the max than 3–4 television monitors, and that those monitors should always be configured to display images in predetermined cycles. When a sensor transmits a signal, the system should automatically switch to the images being sent from the related cameras.

Audio Security

In establishing physical security protection for a facility, audio security (through sound attenuation) should also be considered. Countermeasures can generally be enhanced by restrictions on classified conversation when and where required. The use and possession of privately-owned equipments such as photographic devices, radios, television sets and tape recorders should be restricted within the facility. If mission critical electronic equipments are necessary, they should first be technically tested for possible surveillance devices and technical security hazards. They should also be required to meet national standards for TEMPEST whenever possible. TEMPEST is the US government standards for limiting electric or electromagnetic radiation emanations from electronic equipments.

Sound Transmission Class (STC) describes the transmission attenuation afforded by various wall materials and other building components. A STC of 30 or better means loud speech can be understood fairly well even though normal speech cannot be easily understood. A STC of 40 or better means loud speech can be heard but would be hardly intelligible. A STC of 50 or better means very loud sounds can be heard only faintly.

Phone Line Security

To prevent phone lines and instruments from being used as clandestine (devices working in secret to conceal an illicit purpose) listening devices, all incoming phone cables and wires which penetrate the facility's perimeter should be designed to enter the facility only through one opening. They must be placed under control at the interior face of the perimeter. All active incoming lines should be accounted for by the number of pairs in use, by phone and extension number, and also by the number of excess/unused pairs in existence. All unused incoming wires should be disconnected and grounded for preventing unauthorized use. Additionally, the number of phone instruments to be installed should be limited to those operationally necessary.

Data storage management and network infrastructure security (NEW TOPIC)

Setting up an Internet Gateway would often involve the need for interconnecting with internal networks in order to allow them to gain access to the gateway service. However, considerable care must be exercised to ensure that interconnecting the network will not degrade or weaken the existing security level to an unacceptable level, or compromise the security of information processed. Hence, the connecting parties must:

● Maintain their own specific security defenses on their network, hosts and systems
● Maintain their own security policy and guidelines, but these policies and guidelines must be aligned with that on the Internet Gateway Set up stringent logical access controls to the Internet Gateway
● Establish security incidents handling and reporting procedures for Internet access and services Advise and train users to observe and follow the related

security policy, guidelines & procedures.

Furthermore, it is recommended that a secure Internet gateway, merely offering Internet access services, must provide the following security functions:

- Firewall for access control
- Packet-filtering Routers for routing traffic and packet filtering
- Intrusion Detection System for logging, monitoring & detecting attacks
- Protection against Computer Virus for computer virus detection and prevention

Firewall configuration, administration and operational procedures should always be well documented. Configuration of multiple firewalls used in parallel (if any) must be identical. Integrity checking of the configuration files of the firewall using checksums should be performed whenever applicable. Log recording and review for the firewall should be done regularly. Backups of the system and configuration files for firewall must be regularly taken. And keep in mind, proper maintenance of user accounts is highly important.

You must be aware that firewall is never the totality of a security solution. There are a number of threats that a firewall cannot protect against, including:

- Denial of service attacks and assure data integrity
- Attacks from unwitting users
- Attacks from computer virus or malicious code

On the other hand you want to know that the boundary between firewall and other security measures is becoming increasingly blurred as firewall manufacturers continuously incorporate additional features. A lot of the modern routers, for example, are having basic firewall functions and features. Always remember, routers should be properly configured to deny all traffic by default, and to allow only permitted traffic to go through. Source routing should be disabled. Logging, backup and other administrative tasks should be properly performed similar to those for the firewall.

Synchronous Data Replication or mirroring refers to the process of copying data from one source to another in which an acknowledgement of the receipt of data at the copy location will be required in order for application processing to continue. Asynchronous

Data Replication does not require acknowledgement of any kind. Electronic Vaulting refers to the back-up procedure of copying changed files and transmitting them to an off-site location via a batch process.

As most of the critical IT equipments are normally housed in a data centre or computer room, careful site preparation of the data centre or computer room is highly important. Site preparation should at the least cover the following aspects:

• Site selection
• Power supply
• Air conditioning and ventilation
• Fire protection and detection
• Water damage and flood control
• Physical entry control

Proper cleaning procedures for the computer room must also be established. Such procedures must include at least the following:

• Regular cleaning of the external surfaces of the peripherals by operators;
• Daily emptying of the waste paper bin;
• Daily vacuum cleaning of the computer room floor;
• Daily mopping of the computer room raised floor (if any);
• Periodic cleaning of the water pipes (if any);
• Periodic cleaning of the in-house partitions, doors, lighting fixture and furniture;
• Periodic inspection and cleaning of the floor void.

You must regularly inspect the computer room to ensure the cleaning procedures are followed. Unused peripherals or equipment should be disposed of or written offs. Hardware or workstation should be well covered when there is any cleaning or maintenance work that causes a lot of dust arouse. Eating and drinking in the computer room should be avoided. Smoking in the computer room must be strictly prohibited.

Regular maintenance and testing should be arranged for all service utilities including air conditioning equipment, fire detection and prevention system, standby power supply system, power conditioning system, water sensing system and temperature sensing system. All maintenance work carried out must be recorded. AND, apart from the service utilities, emergency exits, locks and alarms must also be regularly checked.

A fire fighting party should be organized in each operating shift with well-defined responsibility assigned. Regular fire drills must be carried out to allow the officers to practice the routines to be followed when fire breaks out.

Proper controls must be implemented when taking IT equipment away from sites. For hand carry type of IT equipment such as laptop computers and mobile devices, you should consider keeping an authorized equipment list and periodically perform inventory check to check the status of such IT equipment. For fixture type of IT equipment, you may want to adopt a check-in check-out process or inventory documentation measures to identify which IT equipment has been taken away.

Proper procedures must be established for the storing and handling of backup media. Backup media containing business essential and/or mission critical information should be stored at a secure and safe location remote from the site of the equipment. Access to the backup media should only be done via a designated staff as far as possible. Movement of media IN/OUT of a library or off-site storage should be properly logged. Unless permission is granted, any staff should not be allowed to leave the computer room with any media. To facilitate the detection of loss of media, the storage rack can indicate some sort of markings/labels at the vacant slot positions. Periodic inventory check would be necessary to detect any loss or destruction. Transportation of backup media/manuals to and from off-site must be properly handled. The cases used for carrying the media should be shockproof, heatproof, water-resistant and should be able to withstand magnetic interference. In addition, there must be consideration on protecting the media from theft, such as through encrypting the data in the storage media splitting the media into multiple parts and transported by different people.

All media containing classified information must be handled strictly in accordance with the established procedures. The construction of external media library must have the same fireproof rating as the computer room. In fact, the rating for fireproof safe for keeping vital media must reach the standard for keeping magnetic media. To safeguard tape contents from being erased when a tape is accidentally mounted for use, all write-permit rings should be removed from the tapes on the tape racks. Physical disposal of computer equipment containing non-volatile data storage capabilities must be checked and examined to ensure all information has been removed. Destruction, overwriting or reformatting of media must be approved and performed with appropriate facilities or techniques.

Fault Tolerance (NEW TOPIC)

The fault tolerance viewpoint of security is that a trustworthy security system should not depend on any single component functioning correctly, because that component can become a weak point or a vulnerability.

Passive redundancy makes use of excess capacity for reducing the impact of component failures. Active redundancy aims to reduce or eliminate performance decline by monitoring the performance of individual device via voting logic that can determine how to reconfigure the individual components for operation to continue. Electrical power systems often rely on power scheduling to dynamically reconfigure active redundancy.

A security system implemented with a single backup is said to have single point tolerant capability. A fail-safe or fail-secure device is something different - it is a device that, in the event of failure, can respond in a way that is not going to cause any harm to other things in the environment.

Standards, regulations and codes (NEW TOPIC)

There are currently many different standards and codes in the security industry. In fact we recommend that you visit this web site for a complete in-depth list:

http://www.fas.org/sgp/othergov/inventory.html

General operational practices for security improvement

Without proper operational procedures your security system would be severely handicapped. The equipments are the hardware of the system, while the procedures can be thought of as the software.

> **NOTE:** The purpose of a Security Manual of Procedures is to serve as a guide for the orderly administration of security affairs. Implementation of the guidelines should produce policies and procedures designed to guide an organization in its continuous striving for security improvement. The guidelines should also be included in the security training effort. When the manual is too extensive, post orders may be more appropriate. Post orders contain specific instructions that are to be followed by each security officer at a specific area.

Visitor Control Policy

All visitors should be escorted by an authorized staff when they are going to sensitive areas. Site tours should be accompanied and should be restricted to non-sensitive areas only. Background checks may be necessary on visiting international groups.

For purpose of Visitor Screening, you should use outdoor and exit door signs to direct all visitors to the entrance they are to enter. Use positive welcoming signs to clearly indicate where you want your visitors to go. All other exterior doors should be locked (except for emergency exits) thus allowing entrance through one single designated entrance.

All visitors should sign-in and receive a badge. All staff should be expected to question people without a badge and invite them to check in. When leaving the facility visitors should first sign out and return the badge.

For high security area, any Visitor requesting access must obtain prior approval. A Visitor Request Form should be submitted to the Access Control Center at least 24 hours prior to the intended visit.

 NOTE: In any case all visitors must possess verifiable, valid photo government identification.

Alarm Response Policy

Alarm Response Protocols for security-related alarms should be established. The staff force should be trained in these protocols to understand their roles and responsibilities. They should be capable of addressing the problem upon receipt of alarm notification.

A comprehensive set of alarm response protocols should provide guidance for identifying false alarms, unverified alarms, and panic/distress alarms. You must realize that excessive false alarms could get you into troubles. The primary concern is that law enforcement officers are subjected to needless danger when the called on to respond to repeated false alarms.

The common strategies for managing false alarms include verified police response, **fining alarm companies**, two call verification of alarms, enhanced management of false alarms, and enhanced public education.

 NOTE: The panic alarm is installed in locations identified as having the potential for life-threatening situations. This kind of alarm would usually require immediate notification to the police and must therefore be under constant controlled by authorized personnel.

Verified response aims at eliminating law enforcement's initial response to automatic alarm systems unless criminal activity is first confirmed. Enhanced Call Verification (ECV) would require that at least 2 calls from the alarm monitoring center be made to determine whether a user error has occurred prior to involving law enforcement.

Doors and windows to critical areas must be properly alarmed so that unauthorized entry will trigger alert. Access control equipments should be tested with a void card and a valid card – you want to know if the system really works as expected. If excessive false alarms are taking place, fix them ASAP.

NOTE: The doors themselves must be built to be strong and reliable. For facilities that are subject to heavy abuse, wood doors (if you have to use wood) should be specified to be solid core wood block. Wood core doors are especially ideal for acoustically sensitive spaces that require a moderate degree of speech privacy.

Not all doors are heavily used though. Low threat severity and low level of protection would be required for doors such as service entrances, platform doors, dormitory exits ...etc.

In terms of Windows, glazing systems will be used both for security and for energy conservation. Reflective fragment retention film laminated glass is especially recommended for purpose of security engineering.

In fact, you HAVE TO evaluate the company's capability in responding to alarms and other incidents. The element of response is critical – failure to respond would make everything meaningless. Your job as the design consultant here would be to make detection and alert as smooth as possible. A simple example – a door lock alone would not suffice for signaling an intrusion. It has to work with a door status monitor (aka Door Status Switches DSS, door contacts, or alarm contacts) such that when the lock is being messed with the security force can be alerted in time.

NOTE: When designing the security alarm system make sure you avoid confusion with other types of alarm. An Evacuation/Fire Alarm would usually consist of one "whooping sound" followed by a pre-recorded message, this sequence repeating until deactivated. An Elevator Alarm would usually be a shrill, continuous bell which is not as loud.

Key Control Policy

A proper key control policy should specify a limit to the number of employees with keys, possibly a ban on providing keys to contractors and a prohibition on the duplication of keys. Periodic and random change of keys should be enforced, and return of all keys from employees when terminating employment should be mandated.

NOTE: Open key systems fail to provide effective real protection due to the fact that duplicates can be made way too easily. To be realistic, a "Do Not Duplicate" stamp on a key doesn't really work... Restricted key system using keyway that is patent-protected would do a better job even though it could be way more expensive.

The use of patented keys that prevent the unauthorized duplication should be recommended. On the other hand, multiple locks hooked together in a daisy chain as a feature for easy access should be discouraged.

People must be made aware that effective key control guidelines require rooms to be kept locked when not in use. Possession of an authorized key should not connotate permission to be in a secured area. Key Control staff and/or other specifically assigned staff should be authorized to seize any unattended key(s) or unauthorized key duplicate(s). Personal locks or hardware should be disallowed in controlled areas. Positions with the ability to authorize a key request or lock re-core must be clearly identified and published, and that all departments should be held responsible for coordinating annual audit of their internal records with Key Control's records.

> NOTE: Frequent rekeying of locks as a security measure can be expensive and time-consuming.

A grand master key is a single key that can allow access to all or most of the spaces in multiple facilities of the same company. Grand master keys should not be frequently issued, and if issued should require the approval of senior management.

> NOTE: When a key holder separates from the company for whatever reason, all key(s) must be returned to those that approved the issuance of the key on or prior to the last day of employment.
>
> The company may reserve the right to withhold payment owed to the key holder until all key(s) are properly returned.

Access Control Policy

Staff access to each facility area should be restricted based on job requirements. Limits to access may be accomplished through key control or through more sophisticated access control systems. The individual to whom keys or access card are issued would be held personally responsible for the keys and their identification card as well as their use, until properly returned. Exterior door keys/access cards could be made available case by case but a precise need must be present and justified in writing and be approved by the department head.

NOTE: The issue of tail gating must be carefully addressed. Anti-tailgating policies that prohibit people from gaining entry to a workplace by following in on the heels of someone should be put in place for building up a strong overall security posture. Don't forget to strictly enforce the policies with the physical presence of security guards and/or turnstile systems.

Highly sensitive areas should be equipped with additional operational controls which should require two-employee identification before allowing access. Simple locks and keys may not be enough to keep a facility secure from unwanted visitors. Controlling access with greater certainty may be achieved with more sophisticated devices.

Electronic locks may have the ability to restrict access to certain individuals basing on specific hours or days, or for a limited period of time. Some even have audit-trail recording functionality that can be helpful in investigating security incidents. To make them work, however, these locks must be hard-wired into a network, which could be costly and complicated. With standalone computer-managed (CM) locks, the device can be networked through using a personal digital assistant to download data from a computer so that hard-wiring would become unnecessary.

Incorporating biometric devices into your physical security system can ensure that the person being allowed entry is actually the authorized person. Hand-geometry systems use the size and shape of the hand and fingers for identity verification. Factors such as length, width, thickness and surface area of the fingers and hand are measured and compared for access control and time-and-attendance applications. It offers high degree of reliability and is suitable for high volume use. Fingerprint readers rely on the unique pattern of the ridges and valleys of the fingerprint characteristics to identify a person, and is ideal primarily for use with smaller populations. In any case, they are costly to implement, and chance for false reject still exists. You must realize that a false reject can just be as much of a problem as a false acceptance.

NOTE: Identity theft through biometrics measures is difficult. As an example, fingerprint spoofing is pretty rare.

NOTE: At the user level, one of the major challenges of biometrics is hardware adoption and the use of a scanner. Generally, acceptance rate for finger scanning is higher than other biometric measures.

Delivery Access Control Policy

Frequent deliveries may present a difficult security challenge. Physically inspection of vehicles before allowing them in should be required. To make this easy you may want to plan a pull out area to stage delivery vehicles right outside of the fence line. You should also request suppliers and/or visitors to provide the manifest and driver name prior to arrival. Unverifiable, unscheduled, or late deliveries/visits should be refused. Detailed logs of deliveries and pick-ups must be maintained.

A vehicle checkpoint area for detaining vehicles for identification may be deployed in a perimeter access control system. Through this area you may screen all vehicles or pedestrians prior to access. For facility with critical assets, consider to have a guardhouse facility located right at the entrance.

NOTE: You should insist on 100% screening of all vehicles with non-credentialed persons. A sallyport is a combination of electrically operated gates or portals, interlocked to prevent more than one gate from opening at a time. It is a good a means for secured, controlled entry through the fence perimeter. It effectively allows entry processing, paperwork review, and driver identification occur all within the sallyport. You may also opt for the use of bollards, jersey barriers, decorative planters, or other vehicle barriers as a side measure. The thing is, if you are to use them, make sure they are made capable of stopping a 4,000 pound vehicle traveling at 30 miles per hour, all done within 3 feet or less.

Other policies

The use of narcotics and alcoholic beverages could produce serious security related problems and should be disallowed inside the facility. Gambling activities when becoming organized could also lead to problems, especially when someone lose money and fail to control oneself emotionally, and should accordingly be prohibited.

Handling Emergency

Generally speaking, there are different approaches to incident response (depending on the situation), but the goals are highly similar. They are:

- Recovering quickly and efficiently from incidents

- Minimizing impact of the incident

- Responding systematically and decreasing the likelihood of reoccurrence

- Balancing operational, continuity and recovery capability

- Dealing with legal issues

You may also devise workaround procedures - alternative procedures that may be of use by a functional business unit to continue operations during temporary and less severe events.

 NOTE: Isolation of the incident scene should begin (and be performed by trained personnel whenever possible) when the emergency is discovered. If the building is endangered, evacuation may become necessary. Roll call refers to the process of identifying that all employees, customers, business partners and visitors ...etc have been safely evacuated.

When evacuation is ordered, all staff should meet at a designated location (the meeting place). An alternate location should be determined if the first choice turns out to be inaccessible.

A head count should be made at the meeting place. The results of the count should be provided to the next higher authority in the emergency chain of command (which is likely the person in charge of the emergency command center). Missing persons must be immediately reported to the emergency command center.

Emergency management activities typically focus on activities that take place immediately AFTER an event. Proper emergency management program typically includes measures to assure the safety of personnel such as evacuation plans and creation of a command center from which emergency procedures can be executed.

> **Important:** **Protecting life is always the number one key concern. HOWEVER, if you are not dealing with life threatening situation then protecting life would not be the right answer.**

The Emergency Response Plan

The first step in preparing for emergency response is to develop an emergency response plan. For the plan you need to prepare a hazard assessment, which covers threats from hazards other than security risks. You need to establish a command structure to indicate who will take charge and what decisions will be allowed to make in an emergency. Leadership in the command structure must be clearly defined. You must also define how communications will be established and maintained for: i, indicating how an emergency event is established; ii, notifying any request for assistance; and iii, notifying the facility's staff what they should do in response to the emergency.

Very importantly, the plan must indicate how to account for the people in the facility (such that it is possible during an evacuation to verify that everyone is safely evacuated). The plan must also provide a method of training persons in how to respond to a sudden emergency.

> **NOTE:** With a tabletop exercise, those in the command structure would work together at a table talking through what they would do in a mock emergency response exercise.
>
> On the other hand, as the ultimate training exercise the emergency response drill should include operation of the facility alarms and staff

> responses to those alarms.

The Emergency Response Team

You may be confused as to who is responsible for what in the case of emergency. Generally speaking, we have three groups of people at work:

- The Emergency Response Team (ERT) - respond first to the emergency event.

- The Contingency Operations Team (COT) - initiate a contingency plan to ensure the recovery and continuation of business critical functions, including setting up an Alternate Facility, initiating Telework options, bringing in emergency equipment and supplies, etc.

- The Business Recovery Team (BRT) - operate during the Recovery Phase.

The Initial Assessment Team (IAT) as part of the Emergency Response Team (ERT) will execute the Disaster Plan for the organization. As the first responders in the event of a crisis or disaster, the IAT will be responsible for issues that will be addressed before the Business Continuity Crisis Management Team (CMT) is activated.

> **Important:**
>
> ❗
>
> The ERT has prime responsibility for declaring and deactivating an emergency situation.
>
> The ERT Team Leader will notify the Crisis Team Leader of any emergency situation for which the ERT is activated.
>
> The Emergency Response Team will report to the CMT.
>
> The ERT Leader should be authorized to call in off-duty facilities employees. After the decision is made each department head or designee should be responsible for notifying their employees. Each department head should maintain a current roster, including telephone numbers, of

their employees.

The Emergency Command Center

Upon being alerted of a disaster, essential employees will report to the Emergency Command Center (ECC, or EOC Emergency Operations Center) immediately and implement the Emergency Plan according to instructions. Note that:

- The ERT Leader should be stationed by the Emergency Command Center.

- The Emergency Command Center must have access to in-house and external telephone lines.

- When necessary the Emergency Command Center shall move to an alternate location (for safety sake).

 NOTE: An ECC should be dedicated to the purpose of ER. It should be sufficiently equipped with communication equipments, reference materials, activity logs and other tools necessary for making timely response to an emergency.

A "serious" ECC for a high risk region should be staffed 24 hours a day, 7 days a week, 365 days year and utilizes multiple overlapping shifts.

Description of a real life ECC:

The purpose of the ECC is to receive reports of emergencies from a variety of sources, allocate resources based on preplanned response criteria, coordinate interagency incident activities, support the incident as needed, provide internal and external information, and document the activity.

The area used for running the ECC should have emergency power for lighting and outlet power. This area should be provided with red emergency telephones that are independent of the normal telephone system, data ports for Internet connections and cable television hook-up. Folding tables and chairs should be set up at the onset of any emergency. There should be access to a locked area that contains equipment to be deployed in the emergency. A back-up ECC location shall be established just in case the primary location becomes unusable.

An Incident Command System (ICS) was specifically for the fire service although its principles can be applied towards almost all types of emergency situations.

The most critical concern in your command center is electrical power. Unstable power is a threat to consistent operations. HOWEVER, electricity can sometimes be a hazard too. You should have an emergency power off switch installed somewhere close to the exit door to prevent your staff from getting electrocuted. One good way to deal with worries on power outage is to use Dual Power Leads – that is, to install power leads from 2 different power substations.

NOTE: You should have standby generators in your command center. The 2 most popular types of generators are Diesel generator and Natural Gas generator.

NOTE: Each department should maintain a disaster box in their area. This box may include items such as the departmental emergency preparedness plans, emergency telephone numbers, a map of the area, flashlight and batteries, portable radio, plastic baggies, first aid kit and the like.

You also need adequate physical protection, especially in the case of emergency. You use physical barriers to protect your assets. Examples include CCTV, guards, and special kind of locks. Do note that if your locks require electricity to operate then some backup measures would be necessary.

Dealing with external agencies

As a qualified PSP, you should meet with emergency management officials to understand what governmental capabilities exist. These officials likely would have information on the nature of risks to which your area is susceptible. Most countries and governments have emergency management agencies that are tasked to advise and assist the population in dealing with a wide range of natural and man-made threats.

 NOTE: After consulting with the PR function, the ERT Team Leader shall assign staff to manage media access to the emergency site. PR shall assign staff to escort media while in the site. Security can be called to support this effort but shall not be assigned as the sole escort.

Security System Procurement and Project Management

Outsource or not

When dealing with the issue of specialization you need to equip yourself with the proper mindset – you need to realize that you cannot and shouldn't do everything all by yourself.

Some government agencies use the "avoidable cost" method for cost comparison, where an external cost estimate is compared to the internal costs that would not incur if the service was contracted rather than done in house. These avoidable costs would usually include all direct costs, as well as any portions of indirect overhead or short-term fixed costs that can be eliminated over the life of a service contract. Using the avoidable cost method can ensure that a decision to outsource would not result in an increase in the overall cost.

For private entities, Value Chain Analysis describes the activities that are often taking place in your business and relates them to an analysis of the competitive strength of your team. The core idea is that you cannot undertake all primary and support activities, that some would have to be outsourced. Most companies do not have their own security expertise so using outside service would be their only option. One best way to look for outside service is through tendering.

> NOTE: Split contract is one which you do some yourself and let an outside party do the rest – kind of partial outsourcing. Experience shows that all sorts of coordination problem can occur and frustration will result. Avoid this type of contract whenever possible.

Outsourcing security solution implementation

If you are to outsource your solution implementation, you should obtain quotes from at least 3 different vendors. Ask for references from their customers. Find out how quickly they can respond to requests for service after installation. Ask about warranties. Ask them what screening they would do on the hiring of alarm installers.

The Tendering process

The main principle of tendering is that there should be open and fair treatment of suppliers, no supplier should be offered an unfair advantage over any other. At the same time, the risk of the purchasing organization must be minimized.

One primary objective here is the minimizing of risk to the purchasing organization. When departments/individuals obtain quotations/tenders from suppliers they (usually and unknowingly) accept to place the company's Official Order subject to the Supplier's terms and conditions (refer to the next section for basic info on contract law).

The Supplier's own terms and conditions are almost certainly referred to somewhere on their quotation either on the front as a specific term of their offer or on the back as an unconditional condition. Unless this is challenged at the earliest stage and the appropriate company's equivalent terms and conditions are established as the agreed terms and conditions to which the order is subject, then you have accepted the Suppliers terms and conditions which may be disadvantageous to the company.

In order to minimize risk to the company it is good practice before asking companies to submit their quotations/tenders to get them to agree in writing to the company's terms and conditions. This way there can be no argument or misunderstanding at a later stage as to who's terms and conditions apply.

OR, explicitly request that a Proposer (i.e. the bidder) must state those standard terms and conditions which the Proposer will expect the company to consider if deviation from the RFP PROPOSAL specifications is expected. Such deviation must be clearly identified by the Proposer, ideally in RED font.

> **NOTE:** A CONFLICT OF INTEREST QUESTIONNAIRE FORM would usually be required when the secueity project is owned by a public entity / governmental entity.

Pre-qualification

You only want qualified entities to bid. therefore, you need to be highly specific on this. Qualifications may include licensing, training, certifications, business history, references…etc. You may contact product manufacturers to find a list of preferred dealers who are often technically competent. Internet search and referrals may also do the job.

RFP, RFI and RFQ

A Request for Proposal (RFP) is sort of an invitation for suppliers to submit a proposal on a specified type of product and/or service. It deals with comprehensive information in addition to prices. Generally you have your RFP well organized and properly indexed before sending to only those approved suppliers or vendors in your list. Having said that, the writer of the RFP must know exactly what he is doing. A problematic RFP will lead to problematic proposals.

For purpose of information clarification and exchange it may be advisable to host a pre-bid conference which looks something like:

Prospective Proposers are encouraged to attend the pre-proposal conference to be held at XXXXXXXX, at XX:XX a.m. on XXXX, XXXXX. The pre-proposal conference will provide the opportunity to review the requirements and intent of the contract documents.

Writing the RFP

The scope of work is the item which needs to be clarified in order for proposals to be accurately made. You want to make this content as clear and as specific as possible. Keep in mind, if you don't specify something, you are effectively giving the Proposers the freedom to choose.

You may start by giving an overall description of the scope, which should look something like:

The scope of this RFP will require the selected Proposer(s) to prepare and assist the company with all aspects of a successful deployment of an integrated Security solution. In addition, the selected Proposer(s) should demonstrate knowledge and experience in dealing with surveillance and security on a large scale.

One good idea for RFP writing is to have a **PURPOSE** section as the first section of the document. Below shows a real life example:

The purpose of this RFP is to select a Proposer(s) with the competencies, expertise and resources necessary to assist the company in effectively integrating and deploying a Security Surveillance System throughout the facility. Proposer(s) will assist in the deployment, implementation and support of the surveillance system. The goal of the system is to provide real time and archived video of internal and external areas of the company's facility. The selected Proposer(s) will work under the direction and supervision of the company's Director of Security Services.

This RFP will require the selected Proposer(s) to prepare and assist the company with all aspects of the deployment of a security surveillance system. The work itself will consist of all aspects of technology implementation for which the company desires to contract with the selected Proposer(s). The company's vision for the surveillance system technology projects calls for the installation of new technology equipment, cameras, software, cabling and services. The proposal, once formally accepted in writing, will serve as the initial agreement between the company and its selected vendor, with possible extension of the agreement to follow for additional facilities.

The above **PURPOSE** section tells broadly what the whole project is all about and what are to be expected. Details may then be provided throughout the rest of the document. You want to provide as much detail as possible as long as security would not be compromised through such disclosure. A DDS, for example, may be attached to the RFP for Proposers to further study.

Types of RFP

A RFP has all the elements of a RFQ but products are not pre-selected. You do not refer to brand and model. Instead you specify the expected performance requirements and let the respondents make the suggestions.

A single phase RFP requires that the respondents get EVERYTHING written and presented in one single bid document, that there would be no second chance. On the other hand, a two phase RFP would ask for technical evaluation at the first phase (the discovery phase) and then a final round which compares the financial terms and other arrangements.

Single phase RFP is good for simple products where cost is the primary concern. Two phase RFP would be a better choice if technical complexity is foreseeable.

Below please find a sample requirement section extracted from a real life RFP:

Sample PROPOSAL SUBMISSION REQUIREMENTS:

Qualified Security Contractors should submit the following information in their proposal:

- A cover letter stating project interest that includes a statement describing why the Proposer is considered qualified to perform the work required

- A X-page maximum description of the Proposer's organization and types of services provided, including any direct experience performing security work for private sector entities

- Names and phone numbers of four (4) client references

- A resume for each Manager or Supervisor who would possibly be assigned to this account

- A cost proposal indicating the cost/hourly rate for Night Time Patrol Services and Stationary Guard Services (please specify different costs for holidays, overtime, emergency services, etc.)

- Contact information for the person authorized to communicate about this request

> **Important:**
> **!**
>
> Proof of liability insurance should be required. A hold harmless clause should be specified as required by the RFP.

In the RFP it is usually specified that the deadline is absolute and proposals received after the due date and time would not be considered. Proposers would have to select a method of delivery that ensures proposals will be delivered to the correct location by the due date and time. It is also advisable to state that the RFP and any following interview processes should in no way be deemed to create a binding contract or agreement of any kind. See below for an example:

The RFP would in no manner obligate the company to the eventual purchase of any services described, implied or which may be proposed until confirmed by a written contract/purchase order.

> **Important:**
> **!**
>
> For large scale long term project you cannot afford to ignore the proposer's financial stability and ability. You would want to find out more on for their sales numbers, financing and funding...etc.

You may want to request that a Bid Bond be submitted by the Proposer along with his bid for a project. It is usually in an amount of around 10% of his total bid. A Bid Bond is a means for providing the project owner with some financial assurance that should this contractor be awarded the project, he will honor the contract. In fact nearly all Public Sector jobs and many private ones require the posting of a bid bond or cashiers check at the time the bid is submitted.

When a Bid Bond is required, a Performance Bond should also be specified. It should be submitted by a Proposer once he is awarded the job. A Performance Bond guarantees contract performance by the contractor, according to the contract specifications, terms and conditions. This guarantee is backed by the surety company's capital and surplus, up to the financial limit of the bond which is often set at 50% to 100% of the full contract amount.

A Payment Bond may deserve your consideration. It guarantees that a contractor will pay certain bills for labor and materials which are associated with this contract. Again, it is backed by the surety for up to the financial limit of the bond.

NOTE:

On paper, make it clear that the Proposers would have to assume sole responsibility for the complete effort required in the RFP. No special consideration would be given after bids are opened because of a Proposer's failure to be knowledgeable of all the requirements of the RFP.

In the real world, Proposers do make mistake sometimes. On a case by case basis, it would not hurt to give some leeway as long as quality is not sacrificed. Equipment substitution could be allowed for flexibility sake, but prior approval must be required.

You may also want to specify a clause on bid withdrawal. Generally speaking, prior to bid opening Proposer's authorized representative may withdraw the RFP any time by written notice or in person. After opening, however, bid pricing will have to remain in effect for, say, 90 days.

Addendum

If it becomes evident that a RFP shall be amended, you should issue a formal written amendment to all known prospective bidders. After the RFP is issued you may make changes in the form of ADDENDUM. You do want the Proposers to sign acknowledgement which affirms that any cost changes due to the changes described by the Addendum has been duly considered and included in the Bid price.

Changes to be proposed after the conclusion of the bidding process may be made in the form of Change Order. In the RFP you should clearly define the acceptable conditions for change order to be issued.

Pricing

Firm fixed price means there is one price which covers all areas of the security project. Maintenance cost and contract would usually be separately provided.

You do need to realize that this price may not reflect the TOTAL COST for the solution. The total cost must include items such as training cost, maintenance cost, replacement cost, logistic cost, consultation cost (your cut if you are a hired external consultant) …etc. The proper budget must be made ready for all these.

RFQ

You may use a Request for Quotation (RFQ) for simpler yet cheaper items where concerns are on price and delivery.

> NOTE: You may use a RFQ when you know exactly what equipments and services are to be acquired. A RFQ is particularly useful for price comparison purpose. You need to supply a detailed written specification, meaning you must do a lot of research works first before releasing the RFQ. As the writer of the RFQ you take full responsibility and risk on product selection, which may not be too desirable.

RFI

Sometimes you may also want to use Request for Information (RFI) to find out about the capability of a seller in terms of offerings, capabilities and strengths. For complex proposals that require bidding, you may want to host pre-bid conferences to ensure the bidding suppliers fully understand your requirements. In fact, pre-bid conferences are highly recommended. You should get members of top management, the company's purchasing agent, as well as representatives from the maintenance department and security department to attend. You moderate the meeting and the purchasing agent deals specifically with details of the bid process.

NOTE: You may use a RFI when your needs cannot be made highly precise and specific. Through the RFI you explain the overall goals, and you expect the respondent to figure out how to get the overall goals accomplished.

For RFI, you may want to clearly state that your company is not in a position to establish that the information which a Proposer submits is a trade secret and that the Proposer must find ways to "protect" the "trade secret" at his own expense.

You may include a "Vendor questions" section. You want to be very specific in your requests for information here. Use this section to ask respondents to describe how their products will meet your project's needs. Ask, say, what support structure and technical architecture is required to make their solution effective for you. You have to be very specific. When you are NOT specific you are going to receive fluff, not accurate information.

Terms and conditions

Sometimes suppliers may not accept in full the company's terms and conditions. If this happens, ask the company to put in writing their objections and suggested amendments, then send their reply to the Purchasing Office who will gladly take up the issues and resolve them on your behalf. Proceed to the next stage only if everything is resolved. Be careful with any Letters of Intent. Unless you explicitly state in the letters that these letters are not legal binding or that the parties that come up with the letters have no authority to legally bind anything, you may be bound.

In general, a company will have certain Financial Procedures that require something like: "…for all purchases of goods or services where the cost is likely to exceed $XXX a minimum of X competitive quotations must be obtained prior to placing the order wherever practicable". This is to ensure that the best interest of the company is protected. Note that:

● For low value orders it is often possible to obtain value for money by reference to existing arrangements at the company. Where no such arrangements are available, purchasers should aim to receive discounts off the Supplier's catalogue/list prices.

● Formal tendering procedures should normally be used for purchases expected to cost in excess of a few thousand dollars. Where tenders are not sought the reasons must be documented and retained with the copy of the purchase order. Only in exceptional circumstances should orders in excess of such a large sum be placed without competitive tendering.

● There should be a specified closing date and time for the submission of tenders, and the opening of the tenders should be witnessed and recorded by at least two members of staff.

 NOTE: Unless strictly necessary you may not want to go for a public bid opening. Opening bid in the private is simple and can give yourself more time for bid examination.

● Tenders should be evaluated against criteria detailed in the invitation to tender, and the evaluation properly documented.

● The Purchasing Office should advise and assist departments in the drawing up of formal written specifications and tender documents.

● Full records of the specifications used, the criteria for evaluating the quotations/tenders (price alone may not be the only criterion) and prices quoted, together with reasons for final choice of supplier must be retained for a period required by the audit function.

● For equipment purchase: due to the high value involved, the use of checklists is strongly recommended. The publication of the Checklists gives the company the opportunity to address the issue of obtaining better value for money in respect of equipment purchases. One checklist is aimed primarily towards those responsible for resource allocation and the assessment of bids for resource (which may be formal committees or, particularly at departmental level, less formal groups). The second checklist is aimed towards departmental purchasers, both those involved directly in equipment purchase and those, such as heads of department, who are responsible for authorizing purchases.

Liabilities, insurance and a hold harmless clause

To protect yourself against legal liability, the following is a MUST:

CONTRACTOR shall procure and maintain for the duration of the AGREEMENT at its sole cost and expense, insurance against claims for injuries to persons or damages to property which may arise from, or in connection with, the performance of the work hereunder by the CONTRACTOR, its agents, representatives, employees or subcontractors.

The kinds of liabilities to be covered should include and should not be limited to Commercial General Liability (bodily injury, personal injury and property damage), Automobile Liability (bodily injury and property damage) and Workers' Compensation and Employers Liability.

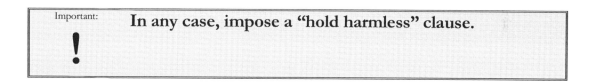

Important:

In any case, impose a "hold harmless" clause.

!

A hold harmless clause may be emphasized via the section on the Independence of Contractor, which should be included in the RFP for saying something like this:

It is understood and agreed that the Contractor (including Contractor's employees) is an independent Contractor and that no relationship of employer-employee exists between the company and the Contractor. The Contractor's assigned personnel shall not be entitled to any benefits payable to employees of the company. The company is not required to make any deductions or withholdings from the compensation payable to Contractor's personnel; and as an independent Contractor, the Contractor agrees to indemnify and hold the company harmless from any and all claims that may be made against the company based upon any contention by any third party that an employer-employee relationship exists by reason of the contract between the company and the Contractor.

If Contractor uses any sub-Contractors, such persons shall be entirely and exclusively under the direction, supervision, and control of the Contractor. All terms of employment, including hours, wages, working conditions, discipline, hiring, and discharging or any other terms of employment or requirements of law, shall be determined by the Contractor. Neither the Contractor nor the Contractor's assigned personnel shall have any entitlement as the employee of the company, right to act on behalf of the company in any capacity whatsoever as agent, nor to bind the company to any obligation whatsoever.

Rights to contracted properties

You should make it clear early in the RFP that the contractor or the contractor's assigned personnel shall not publish or disseminate information gained through participation in their contract(s) without specific prior review and written consent by your company. All materials originated, developed, used or obtained in the performance of contracted services shall remain the property of your company and shall be delivered to your company upon request.

Contract mechanism

For the purposes of proper contracting, you want to look briefly at business law governing simple contracts. A contract may be defined as a communicated agreement between two parties, enforceable at law, whereby the parties promise to do or refrain from doing, some specified act or acts. The three essentials of a contract are:

- an offer by one party and acceptance by another;

- genuine agreement between the parties; and

- the presence of consideration.

A contract does not have to take any particular form, or even have to be in writing, to be binding (still, in writing avoids misunderstanding). An official purchase order with its stated terms and conditions issued in response to a quotation or tender can create a valid contract. Furthermore, the existence of a contract can be inferred from the actions of the parties - for example, the acceptance and use of goods will normally create an obligation to pay for them, even if they were unsolicited.

Once an offer has been made and accepted, a contract is brought into existence. However, an offer may be withdrawn at any time before acceptance. Acceptance must be made by the time stipulated in the offer. If no time is stated the offer must be accepted within a reasonable time. What is reasonable is governed by circumstances, but it should be remembered that a slow or late acceptance may be met by dispute as to whether the original offer is still valid.

Offer and acceptance may be made by any suitable means of communication unless the offerer has stipulated otherwise. The contract comes into existence when the acceptance is received by the offerer except when the post is used. In this case, the contract is deemed to come into existence when the acceptance is posted, provided that it is addressed to the offerer's usual place of business or such address as may be stipulated in the offer. Nowadays it is not uncommon to use FAX or Email as the mean of communication. They are all legally acceptable (for email, digital signatures are required if you want to be 100% ok).

The acceptance must be absolute and identical with the offer. Any material variations between offer and acceptance, or any conditional acceptance, constitutes a counter-offer. This in turn must be accepted unconditionally by the original offerer before a contract exists. It is important to recognize that any counter-offer included in an acknowledgement of an order will be binding if the counter-offer is accepted.

Where a supplier has made an offer and clarification of the offer or negotiation of terms is needed, the purpose and scope of the discussion should be made clear at the outset, as should the fact that any agreements arrived at are subject to ratification by the appropriate delegate. Any variation to the offer arising from such discussions should be put in writing by the offerer and treated as an amendment to the offer.

Once a contract is created it cannot normally be revoked or amended unilaterally. However a contract can be amended any number of times, or revoked, by mutual agreement by the parties (this part is better done in writing to avoid future disputes).

Consideration refers to the presence of reciprocal undertakings by the parties. In the present context it will usually refer to the supply goods or services in return for the payment of money. However, money is not the only form of consideration, for example, where there is an exchange or trade-in of goods. It is not relevant to the validity of the contract whether the consideration is, or appears to be, adequate recompense to the other party.

In a contract, there must be evidence of a clear understanding by the parties as to their intentions. The existence of a misunderstanding of material matters by one of the parties may void the contract. However, this contingency is limited by law to mistakes as to the nature of the transaction, its subject matter, or the identity of the other party.

Following from the description of offers and counter offers above the normal rule is that the terms and conditions attached to the last exchange of paper will apply to the contract. Departments should always seek to make purchases in accordance with the company's terms and conditions. However a supplier's acknowledgement of a purchase order may re-impose the supplier's terms and conditions, in which case the department should reply briefly to remind the supplier that the company's terms and conditions will apply.

A contract is said to be discharged when no obligation remains to be fulfilled. It may be discharged by:

- performance of the agreed obligations by both parties;

- mutual agreement, if neither party has performed its obligations;

- impossibility of performance; or

- breach of contract.

In the event of a party failing to fulfill its contractual obligations, the remedies available to the other party include the following:

- If the contract is incapable of further performance, the other party may sue for damages for any loss suffered, and be released from performance of its own contractual obligations.

- If the contract is still capable of fulfillment but a major breach has occurred, the other party may treat the contract as being at an end, sue for damages and be released from performance of its obligations; or may treat the contract as continuing and sue for damages for any loss suffered.

- If the contract is still capable of fulfillment and a major breach has not occurred, the other party may sue for damages but may not be released from its contractual obligations.

- In some areas of contracting, it is possible to sue for specific performance - that is, to force the other party to complete the contract. However in some instances a term can be incorporated into the Contract where the buyer's remedy is to buy elsewhere and to recover any extra costs from the defaulting party.

It is possible for the parties to a contract to include special provisions to cover default and/or the payment of liquidated damages. However, liquidated damage clauses, although often useful, may serve to severely and unreasonably limit the liabilities of the supplier and should be approached with caution.

NOTE: You may want to address the use of escalation procedures under potential default conditions.

Contract Administration

Contract Administration involves those activities performed after a contract has been awarded to determine how well the purchasing organization and the contractor performed to meet the requirements of the contract. It encompasses all dealings between the purchasing organization and the contractor from the time the contract is awarded until the work has been completed and accepted or the contract terminated, payment has been made, and disputes have been resolved. As such, contract administration constitutes that primary part of the procurement process that assures the purchasing organization gets what it paid for.

In contract administration, the focus is on obtaining supplies and services, of requisite quality, on time, and within budget. While the legal requirements of the contract are determinative of the proper course of action of purchasing organization officials in administering a contract, the exercise of skill and judgment is often required in order to protect effectively the buy side interest.

The specific nature and extent of contract administration varies from contract to contract. It can range from the minimum acceptance of a delivery and payment to the contractor to extensive involvement by program, audit and procurement officials throughout the contract term. Factors influencing the degree of contract administration include the nature of the work, the type of contract, and the experience and commitment of the personnel involved. Contract administration starts with developing clear, concise performance based statements of work to the extent possible, and preparing a contract administration plan that cost effectively measures the contractor's performance and provides documentation to pay accordingly.

NOTE: A punch list should be used to list all project items that are left to be fixed by the contractor.

Post award orientation, either by conference, letter or some other form of communication, should be the beginning of the actual process of good contract administration. This communication process can be a useful tool that helps purchasing organization and contractor achieve a clear and mutual understanding of the contract requirements, helps the contractor understand the roles and responsibilities of the purchasing organization officials who will administer the contract, and reduces future problems. It is helpful to have a pre-meeting with applicable program and contracting officials prior to the post award orientation conference so that there is a clear understanding of their specific responsibilities and restrictions in administering the contract.

Items that should be discussed at the pre-meeting include such things as the authority of purchasing organization personnel who will administer the contract, quality control and testing, the specific contract deliverable requirements, special contract provisions, the purchasing organization's procedures for monitoring and measuring performance, contractor billing, voucher approval, and payment procedures.

Ethics in contracting (NEW TOPIC)

These are some general ethical guidelines:

- Strive to attain the highest professional standard of job performance, to exercise diligence in carrying out the duties of his or her employer, and to serve that employer to the best of one's ability.

- Keep informed of acquisition developments, through academic course work and attendance at symposia, in order to increase knowledge, skill and thoroughness of work preparation.

- Respect the confidence and trust reposed in the member by one's employer.

- Conduct oneself in such a manner as to maintain trust and confidence in the integrity of the acquisition process.

- Avoid engagement in any transaction that might conflict with the proper discharge of one's employment duties by reason of a financial interest, family relationship, or any other circumstance causing a breach of confidence in the acquisition process.

- Not knowingly influence others to commit any act that would constitute a violation of ethical codes.

Vendor prequalification and bid evaluation (NEW TOPIC)

Supplier pre-qualification is usually carried out as part of the due diligence process to evaluate suppliers.

A prequalification questionnaire may request for information on things like:

- the applicants details;

- the details of products and/or services the applicant is seeking to provide;

- the applicants organization structure and ownership;

- the applicants quality management policy and any quality certifications held;

- the contracts undertaken by the applicant over the last X years;

- the environmental, ethics and occupational health and safety policies;

- the audited financial statements for the last X years.

Site visits may be necessary and may cover the evaluation of:

- the location of the suppliers business premises;

- whether or not the applicant is duly registered and licensed;

- the competence of management and applicants technical skills;

- the condition of the suppliers premises and production process;

- the ethical and environmental conditions;

- the existence of standard quality compliance programs.

The Source Selection Plan (SSP) is a key document for specifying how the source selection activities will be organized, initiated, and conducted. It is going to serve as the guiding document for conducting the evaluation and analysis of proposals, as well as the selection of source(s) for the acquisition. You may think of it as a blueprint for conducting the source selection.

To successfully executed, the SSP must clearly and succinctly express the evaluation factors and their relative order of importance. In other words, it ensures that the procuring organization can and will conduct a fair evaluation based upon the stated criteria, which is usually found in Section M of the RFP.

Selecting the appropriate evaluation factor is a highly important step in the entire source selection process. Evaluation factors and sub-factors must be intimately related to the requirement and must be tailored to the acquisition at hand. Sub-factors that result in pass/fail evaluations should be discouraged. Also, since it is not really practical to evaluate every aspect of the requirements for a complex project, only those that have the potential for identifying differences between offerors should be considered. Simply put, evaluation factors and criteria should address those aspects of performance most critical to project success. They should be limited to discriminators where one offeror can really distinguish itself from another in their proposed approach.

Goods and services which are typically suitable for repetitive needs may better be procured through restricted tendering, provided the goods and services have been originally provided through a competitive process. Under this procedure, bids may still be invited, but primarily from which had submitted responsive bids for the earlier purchase order or contract. In some exceptional cases, if the winning bid was clearly superior to the other bids in terms of price, reliability and performance, the additional items, may actually be procured instead by placing a repeat order with the supplier which provided the same items previously, provided the price to be paid for the repeat order is not more than the original price. The repeat order should, however, follow the earlier order within a specified time limit and that the additional quantities should normally not exceed the original quantities.

Vendors of record are used to reduce costs by establishing strategic relationships with a small group of suppliers. A VOR can also be called a preferred suppliers list, with the premise being that organizations should try to focus as much procurement spend as possible through their VOR or preferred suppliers, where typically the best price is achieved.

Organizations may also establish organization-specific VOR arrangements for the supply of a certain category of goods, services or construction. Do note that a VOR arrangement would require a second-stage selection process to assist purchasing organizations in obtaining best value for money.

The first step in a typical bid evaluation process is to ascertain whether submissions are compliant. Submissions may be considered to be materially compliant, but certain clarifications may be sought. On the other hand, materially non-compliant submissions would be rejected. Proponents may be asked for clarification on their bid as long as it does not change their bid in any way.

Where bids are received in response to a solicitation but exceed the organization's budget, are not responsive to the requirement or do not represent fair market value, a revised solicitation may be issued in an effort to obtain an acceptable bid. If unfortunately no bids are acceptable and it is not reasonable to go through any other method, direct negotiation with a chosen supplier may be allowed.

Be extremely careful on the issue of discrimination. Organizations that make decisions based on discrimination may be subject to bid protests or disputes from those feeling that the process may have been biased. All qualified suppliers must be informed through the call for competition of the existence of any specific preference and the rules applicable to those. Also pay particular attention to:

● The biasing of technical specifications in favor of, or against, particular goods or services;

● The timing of events in the competitive process so as to prevent suppliers from submitting bids;

● The specification of quantities and delivery schedules of a scale and frequency that may reasonably be judged as deliberately designed to prevent suppliers from meeting the requirements of the procurement;

● The use of price discounts or preferential margins to favor particular suppliers.

Configuration Management

Configuration management (CM) refers to the field of management with heavy focuses on establishing and maintaining consistency of a security system's performance and its functional and physical attributes with the relevant requirements, design, and operational information throughout its life. Serviceability of a system may be defined in terms of the amount of usage the component has had since installed, since repaired, the amount of use it has had over its useful life (and may be some other limiting factors).

Warranty (NEW TOPIC)

You want to know that the principal purposes of a warranty are to delineate the rights and obligations of the contractor for defective items and services; and to foster quality performance. Generally, a warranty would provide a contractual right for the correction of defects notwithstanding any other requirement of the contract pertaining to acceptance of the supplies or services; and a stated period of time or use, or the occurrence of a specified event, after acceptance to assert a contractual right for the correction of defects.

Generally, the contractor's obligations under warranties would extend to all defects discovered during the warranty period, but would not include damage caused by the buyer. When a warranty for the entire item is not advisable, a warranty may be required for a particular aspect of the item that may require special protection. If the buyer specifies the design of the end item and its measurements, tolerances, materials, tests, or inspection requirements, the contractor's obligations for correction of defects would usually be limited to defects in material and workmanship or failure to conform to specifications. If the buyer does not specify the design, the warranty may extend to the usefulness of the design. If express warranties are included in a contract, all implied warranties of merchantability and fitness for a particular purpose would be negated by the use of specific language in the clause.

Normally, a warranty would allow the buyer to obtain an equitable adjustment of the contract, or direct the contractor to repair or replace the defective items at the contractor's expense. If it is not practical to direct the contractor to make the repair or replacement, the warranty may provide alternate remedies, such as retaining the defective item and reducing the contract price by an amount equitable under the circumstances; or arranging for the repair or replacement of the defective item by another source at the contractor's expense.

CSI standards (NEW TOPIC)

The Construction Specifications Institute (CSI) is in a position to produce construction language standards for building specification. It's MasterFormat is believed to be the most widely used system for organizing construction project manuals in the US. It is basically a system for organizing construction information into procurement and contracting requirements, as well as technical divisions of activities and work practices. It serves well as a framework of the master list of numbers and titles classified by work results or construction practices.

Project Management (NEW TOPIC)

The Project time management discipline has evolved from simple timelines to Gantt charts to product evaluation and review technique (PERT) and critical path method (CPM) tools.

A critical path describes the sequence of project network activities with the longest overall total duration. It is possible for a project to have multiple parallel near critical paths.

Timetables detailing the project tasks and the time or resources necessary to complete them are generally too simplistic for large complicated projects. Gantt charts that are primarily used to visually indicate the duration of each activity are relatively easy to read and monitor progress, but are quite difficult to reschedule and do not allow for prediction of problems.

CPM can be used to ensure that the logic of the plan is accurate, thus being able to provide measure of importance for each task and create a graphical display useful for task control. With CPM you want to construct a model of your project that includes a list of all activities required to complete the project, the time it takes for each activity to complete, and the dependencies between all these activities. You then identify the critical path. The idea is simple. Let's say you need to complete a project earlier than your Critical Path Analysis says is possible. You may want to cut down the length of time spent on your project stages. You may do so by piling resources into every project activity, but this could lead to high overhead. A better option would be to focus only on activities on the critical path. Tune those activities and you may come up with better options.

PERT is often being perceived as a variation of CPM. PERT has a more skeptical view of the time needed for completing each project stage. PERT networks emphasize milestones (i.e. task completions) over total project time. PERT networks can be used to describe projects mathematically as jobs, events, and lengths of duration, thus allowing the determination of the shortest path through the project.

When using PERT you will come across the following terms. Optimistic time refers to the minimum possible time required to accomplish a task, assuming everything proceeds better than expected. Pessimistic time refers to the maximum possible time required to accomplish a task when everything goes wrong. Most likely time talks about the best estimate of the time required to accomplish a task when things don't go too good nor too bad. The time to use for each project stage may be calculated as follow:

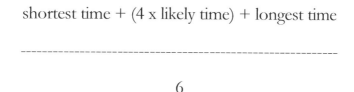

$$\frac{\text{shortest time} + (4 \times \text{likely time}) + \text{longest time}}{6}$$

OR   (Optimistic + 4 x Most Likely + Pessimistic)/6

The Critical Path in PERT is the longest possible path taken from the initial starting event to the terminal event. Any time delays along this path can delay the reaching of the terminal event by the same amount of time. Lag time describes the earliest possible time by which a successor event can follow a specific PERT event. The slack of an event refers to the measure of excess time and resources available in achieving an event. You may be happy to see positive slack as it indicates ahead of schedule.

PERT makes the assumption that events are taking place in a logical sequence and that no activity can commence until its immediately preceding event is fully completed.

The primary drawback of PERT and CPM is that since estimations are used in the calculation of times, the whole analysis could be flawed if a single yet significant mistake is made in estimating any of the involved values.

There are three methods for employing CPM/PERT. The first two methods may be easily employed in small projects with limited scopes. The third method may be used with projects of any size:

- The enumeration method, which finds all possible paths and selects the shortest.

- The work-on-the-diagram method, which uses the visual representation of the network to find shortest path through the network.

- The two-pass tubular, which connects all zero slack time activities so that the critical path may be isolated.

As a popular alternative to critical path analysis, the Critical Chain Project Management (CCPM) method is based on methods and algorithms derived from Goldratt's theory of constraints. A critical chain comprises a sequence of both precedence- and resource-dependent terminal elements. Implicit resource dependencies are assumed, and that emphasis is on finding a good enough solution rather than an optimal solution. Buffers such as project buffer, feeding buffers and resource buffers are also frequently used.

 NOTE: To compress a schedule you may either crash it (by adding more resources) or fast track it (by doing things in parallel). In any case your focus has to be on the critical path tasks.

Practice Review Questions

Practice Question 1:

When facing risk, the typical strategic choices should include (choose all that apply):

A. Terminate the activity giving rise to risk

B. Transfer risk to another party

C. Reduce risk by using of appropriate control measures or mechanisms

D. Accept the risk

E. None of the choices.

Answer: ABCD

Practice Question 2:

Which of the following is a term that describes the processes and procedures an organization puts in place to ensure that essential functions can continue during and after a disaster?

A. BCP

B. DRP

C. CRP

D. ER

E. Risk Assessment

Answer: A

Practice Question 3:

From a physical security point of view, what would refer to a systematic analysis of the facilities assets and an assessment of the vulnerability of those assets from different types of threats?

A. BCP

B. DRP

C. CRP

D. ER

E. Risk Assessment

Answer: E

Practice Question 4:

Criteria for the design of security systems should always be based on the identification of:

A. business assets that may become potential targets

B. critical business assets that may or may not become potential targets

C. business assets that may or may not become potential targets

D. critical business assets that may become potential targets

E. None of the choices.

Answer: D

Practice Question 5:

Risk is the product of:

A.   threat and assets.

B.   assets and mitigations.

C.   losses and prevention.

D.   threat and vulnerability.

E.   None of the choices.

Answer: D

Practice Question 6:

Which of the following is typically defined as an event of low probability yet highly damaging that really catches your attention?

A.   Threat

B.   Risk

C.   Loss

D.   Issue

E.   Emergency

F.   Vulnerability

Answer: A

Practice Question 7:

Which of the following are the possible threats to facilities (choose all that apply):

A.   property loss

B.   violence

C.   unauthorized access

D.   lost persons

E.   None of the choices.

Answer: ABCD

Practice Question 8:

Facilities highly visible to protest groups or terrorist groups are always subject to the threat of:

A.   environmental hazards

B.   property loss

C.   violence

D.   lost persons

E.   None of the choices.

Answer: A

Practice Question 9:

Threat from criminals may NOT include (choose all that apply):

A. theft

B. burglary

C. vandalism

D. sabotage

E. arson

F. None of the choices.

Answer: F

Practice Question 10:

Which of the following correctly describes the intent of terrorists?

A. to disrupt operations through destroying the assets.

B. to steal properties.

C. to recover losses.

D. to arson.

E. None of the choices.

Answer: A

Practice Question 11:

For criminal threats what would be one good source of data?

A. Uniform Crime Report

B. Uniform Labor Report

C. Uniform Police Report

D. Uniform Terrorist Report

E. None of the choices.

Answer: A

Practice Question 12:

Which of the following is a concept that provides the information necessary for designing a physical protective system to detect and delay an attack for the most probable adversary.?

A. RBT

B. CBT

C. ADT

D. DBT

E. None of the choices.

Answer: D

Practice Question 13:

Identification of which of the following should be regarded as a major management decision that requires the input of various operational and management level personnel?

A. RBT

B. CBT

C. ADT

D. DBT

E. None of the choices.

Answer: D

Practice Question 14:

Which of the following is usually defined as a weakness that is exploited in some very negative way?

A. Threat

B. Risk

C. Loss

D. Issue

E. Emergency

F. Vulnerability

Answer: F

Practice Question 15:

Which of the following is an activity which assesses a business function's security vulnerability based on its criticality to the organization's overall business objectives?

A. Criticality analysis

B. Risk analysis

C. Threat analysis

D. Vulnerability analysis

E. Vulnerability assessment

F. None of the choices.

Answer: A

Practice Question 16:

In the security industry, the formal technical definition of which of the following is the evaluation of characteristics that contribute to and mitigate the susceptibility of an asset to damage or weakness that can be exploited by an aggressor?

A. Criticality analysis

B. Risk analysis

C. Threat analysis

D. Vulnerability assessment

E. None of the choices.

Answer: D

Practice Question 17:

Developing a vulnerability assessment would involve defining a list of vulnerabilities and potential improvements that are properly ranked according to:

A. the potential risk.

B. the asset value.

C. the potential criticality.

D. the potential damage.

E. None of the choices.

Answer: A

Practice Question 18:

Which of the following are usually expressed in the form of concentric circles surrounding each asset, with each succeeding circle widening?

A. Fencing

B. Security Gates

C. Intrusion Detection Boundary

D. Physical security perimeters

E.   None of the choices.

Answer: D

Practice Question 19:

You should make use of which of the following for identifying assets that are to be protected (choose all that apply):

A.   floor plans

B.   plot plans

C.   building codes

D.   fire codes

E.   None of the choices.

Answer: A B

Practice Question 20:

A cost-benefit analysis would be most robust if the relevant benefits can be:

A.   quantified

B.   graphically described

C.   described in plain text

D.   easily forecasted.

E.   None of the choices.

Answer: A

Practice Question 21:

A vulnerability assessment for physical security must consider:

A.   attack frequencies

B.   attack detection

C.   attack characterization

D.   the routes and means used to attack

E.   None of the choices.

Answer: D

Practice Question 22:

Which of the following is NOT a critical corporate asset to protect?

A.   labor force

B.   corporate knowledge

C.   business plans

D.   information servers

E.   None of the choices.

Answer: D

Practice Question 23:

A finding of negligence for damages stemming from a security breach would usually require (choose all that apply):

A. reasonable ability to foresee the damages

B. a duty to the injured person

C. actual violation of the duty

D. possible violation of the duty

E. None of the choices.

Answer: A B C

Practice Question 24:

The major models for loss calculation are (choose all that apply):

A. SLE

B. ALE

C. CLE

D. ELE

E. None of the choices.

Answer: A B C

Practice Question 25:

Which of the following loss calculation model would approach risks by taking into account all of the bad things that are likely to happen to your business over the next year?

A. SLE

B. ALE

C. CLE

D. ELE

E. None of the choices.

Answer: C

Practice Question 26:

Which of the following refers to the evaluation of the strengths and weaknesses of your company's disaster preparedness and the impact an interruption would have on your business?

A. BIA

B. RA

C. RM

D. ERP

E. None of the choices.

Answer: A

Practice Question 27:

Which of the following are the primary goals of BIA (choose all that apply):

A. Criticality Prioritization

B. Downtime Escalation

C. Resource Requirement Identification

D. Risk Management

E. None of the choices.

Answer: A B C

Practice Question 28:

It is important for background checks to get completed:

A. prior to job offers are being made.

B. after a job offer is confirmed.

C. when a candidate is hired.

D. when a staff is dismissed.

E. None of the choices.

Answer: A

Practice Question 29:

Stakeholders that will most likely be involved in emergency responses include (choose all that apply):

A. Internal groups

B. External groups

C. External agencies

D. Media

E. None of the choices.

Answer: A B C D

Practice Question 30:

Which of the following are commonly used by fire and police departments for emergency communication?

A. 700 MHz radios

B. 900 MHz radios

C. 800 MHz radios

D. 600 MHz radios

E. None of the choices.

Answer: C

Practice Question 31:

In order to enable an organization to respond to and recovery from disruptive and destructive information security events, the security professional should aid in the planning and performance of which of the following tasks (choose all that apply):

A. Develop and implement process for detecting, identifying and analyzing security-related events

B. Develop response and recovery plans that include organizing, training and equipping the teams

C. Ensure periodic testing of the response and recovery plans where appropriate

D. Ensure the execution of response and recover plans as required

E. None of the choices.

Answer: A B C D

Practice Question 32:

Which of the following are the valid incident response goals (choose all that apply):

A. Recovering quickly and efficiently from security incidents

B. Minimizing impact of the security incident

C. Responding systematically and decreasing the likelihood of reoccurrence

D. Dealing with legal issues

E. None of the choices.

Answer: A B C D

Practice Question 33:

To effectively plan for security specific Incident Handling, you cannot afford to miss which of the following steps (choose all that apply):

A.   Come up with a clear, concise statement of scope.

B.   Provide business resource descriptions.

C.   Perform an impact assessment.

D.   Delegate roles and responsibilities

E.   None of the choices.

Answer: A B C D

Practice Question 34:

With the ABCD Model, what would be the major functions of DETERRENTS (choose all that apply):

A.   surveillance

B.   intelligence

C.   enforcement

D.   backup

E.   None of the choices.

Answer: A B

Practice Question 35:

Give the comment below:

"The trend is for the security force to focus more on response but less on D D D".

What does "DDD' cover (choose all that apply):

A. deterrence

B. detection

C. delay

D. decommission

E. None of the choices.

Answer: A B C

Practice Question 36:

Give the comment below:

"The trend is for the security force to focus more on response but less on D D D".

Is this true?

A. True

B. False

C. True only for small scale facility

D. True only for large scale facility

E. True only for facility in areas of low crime level

F. True only for facility in areas of high crime level

Answer: A

Practice Question 37:

The weakness link of any access control system would be:

A. door locks

B. windows

C. key pads

D. people

E. None of the choices.

Answer: D

Practice Question 38:

Integrated physical security (IPS) consists of the mutually supporting elements of (choose all that apply):

A. perimeter network management

B. physical security measures

C. operational procedures

D. security policies

E. None of the choices.

Answer: B C D

Practice Question 39:

Which of the following refers to the process recommended to be implemented with IPS?

A. DDDRRR

B. DDDSSD

C. DRDDSD

D. DSSERT

E. None of the choices.

Answer: A

Practice Question 40:

Rate this comment: "In any case the strength of the latch and frame anchor should equal that of the door and frame".

A. This is always true security-wise

B. true only for wooden door

C. true only for door with wooden frame

D. true only for metal door

E.   true only for door with metal frame

F.   true only for door with aluminum frame

Answer: A

Practice Question 41:

To provide multiple layers of defense, you should have perimeter intrusion detection mechanisms placed at which of the following locations (choose the single best answer):

A.   the inner edges of the asset boundary

B.   the outer edges of the asset boundary

C.   the access gate

D.   the side windows

E.   None of the choices.

Answer: B

Practice Question 42:

Which of the following refers to the distance between an asset and a threat?

A.   safety distance

B.   monitor distance

C.   intrusion distance

D.   standoff distance

E. None of the choices.

Answer: D

Practice Question 43:

Which of the following are the proper guidelines to follow concerning doors (choose all that apply):

A. doors should be located in well-lighted area

B. if steel based door is not an option, do NOT use door made of aluminum alloy or solid-core hardwood.

C. double doors should be secured with multiple-point long flush bolts.

D. door hinges should use removable pins.

E. None of the choices.

Answer: A C

Practice Question 44:

What is the weakest part of most door assemblies?

A. the latching component.

B. the lock.

C. the pins.

D. the frame.

E.   None of the choices.

Answer: A

Practice Question 45:

As recommended by FEMA, exterior doors should open outward and hinges should be located:

A.   on a door's exterior

B.   on a door's interior

C.   on a door's latch.

D.   on a door's lock.

E.   None of the choices.

Answer: B

Practice Question 46:

Which of the following may best be prepared using spreadsheet?

A.   DDS

B.   ADA

C.   OSHA

D.   DDDRRR

E.   None of the choices.

Practice Question 47:

Design specifications are generally divided which major parts (choose all that apply):

A. General

B. Products

C. Execution

D. Summary

E. None of the choices.

Practice Question 48:

Which of the following is necessary for determining the security level of the facility and the minimum-security safeguards required for protecting personnel and assets?

A. logical security survey

B. physical security survey

C. crime analysis at the tactical level

D. crime analysis at the strategic level

E. crime analysis at the global business level

F. None of the choices.

Answer: B

Practice Question 49:

Which of the following is ALWAYS the first line of defense in providing physical security?

A. Perimeter protection

B. Interior controls

C. Intrusion detection

D. Intrusion deterrent

E. None of the choices.

Answer: A

Practice Question 50:

Open key systems fail to provide effective real protection due to what reason?

A. key management is complicated.

B. key can be broken too easily.

C. duplicates can be made way too easily.

D. key pads are not secure.

E. None of the choices.

Answer: C

Practice Question 51:

What is the drawback of using sequential switching?

A. no alarm is allowed.

B. alarm mode is not supported.

C. the viewer can only view one output at a time.

D. resolution is poor.

E. None of the choices.

Answer: C

Practice Question 52:

With a sequential switch the video signals from each camera are switched in random sequence.

A. True

B. False

Answer: B

Practice Question 53:

If tape based VCR is preferred, to save tape space you should consider to use:

A. time-lapse recorders

B. screen-less recorders

C. mode-less recorders

D. button-less recorders

E. None of the choices.

Answer: A

Practice Question 54:

If lossy compression is the only option for video recording, be sure to turn on:

A. page-mode

B. alarm-mode

C. full screen mode

D. half screen mode

E. None of the choices.

Answer: B

Practice Question 55:

Disk based DVR should be configured to record each frame at a minimum resolution of:

A. 320 x 480 pixels.

B.   1024 x 480 pixels.

C.   640 x 480 pixels.

D.   1640 x 1480 pixels.

E.   None of the choices.

Answer: C

Practice Question 56:

Analog VCRs should be configured to record each image at a minimum line resolution of:

A.   240 visible lines.

B.   340 visible lines.

C.   290 visible lines.

D.   270 visible lines.

E.   None of the choices.

Answer: A

Practice Question 57:

A monitor capable of operating in an under-scan mode is NEVER recommended.
A.   True

B.   False

Answer: B

Practice Question 58:

For serious security effort, wireless camera should be highly encouraged.

A. True

B. False

Answer: B

Practice Question 59:

The exit cameras should be aimed toward the interior.

A. True

B. False

Answer: A

Practice Question 60:

Exterior cameras that are intended to record images of vehicles must be placed in such a way capable of providing direct views of the vehicle so that _____ can be made clearly visible.

A. the driver's face

B. the driver's back

C. the license plate

D. the passengers' faces

E. None of the choices.

Answer: C

Practice Question 61:

What would be true about the number and placement of cameras?

A. they must be sufficient to provide adequate coverage and detail in the monitored area.

B. they must be within quarterly budget.

C. they must be registered with the local police department.

D. they must be of the same make.

E. None of the choices.

Answer: A

Practice Question 62:

When selecting the cameras to use, consideration should be given to:

A. any need for recording audio with the video from one or more cameras.

B. the file format to use.

C. the audio sample frequency to use.

D. the compression mode supported

E. None of the choices.

Answer: A

Practice Question 63:

You may use which of the following units to pivot the cameras?

A. RTZ

B. YTZ

C. XTZ

D. PTZ

E. None of the choices.

Answer: D

Practice Question 64:

Infrared lighting may be used to provide:

A. improved low light performance for monochrome cameras.

B. heat detection for monochrome cameras.

C. alarm mode lighting for monochrome cameras.

D. compress mode lighting for monochrome cameras.

E. None of the choices.

Answer: A

Practice Question 65:

High pressure sodium lights are NEVER the good sources of lighting.

A. true

B. false

Answer: B

Practice Question 66:

Poor lighting cannot degrade the quality of video images.

A. true

B. most of the time true

C. false

Answer: C

Practice Question 67:

Generally speaking, a door that opens into the protected space is more secure than one that opens out.

A.   True

B.   False

Answer: A

Practice Question 68:

Openings in buildings may be divided into the major categories of (choose all that apply):

A.   doors

B.   windows

C.   ventilation

D.   utility openings

E.   None of the choices.

Answer: A B C D

Practice Question 69:

Video motion detector (VMD) works by comparing:

A.   grey scale levels.

B.   image shapes.

C. image angles.

D. heat levels.

E. None of the choices.

Answer: A

Practice Question 70:

Recordings that depict criminal activity have to be preserved with:

A. a check sheet.

B. a documented chain of custody.

C. a sign off sheet.

D. a certificate.

E. None of the choices.

Answer: B

Practice Question 71:

Possible sources of noise that could affect video quality may include (choose all that apply):

A. poor circuit design

B. heat

C. over-amplification

D. automatic gain control

E. transmission systems

Answer: A B C D E

Practice Question 72:

Fence fabric should be of a one-piece form and should be coated with:

A. zinc or polyvinyl chloride.

B. stainless steel.

C. tin or zinc.

D. paint or rubber.

E. None of the choices.

Answer: A

Mock Test on Physical Security

Try to time yourself for the mock test. To give yourself sufficient time to review your answers upon completion, you should spend on average one minute or less on each question.

To ensure technical accuracy, we create the physical security questions referencing the following authentic sources:

● The Complete Guide for CPP (Muuss and Rabern, 2006)

● Contemporary Security Management (Fay, 2002)

● Physical Security and the Inspection Process (Roper, 1997)

1, Examples of physical security access control may include (choose all that apply):

A.   human guard

B.   mechanical lock

C.   CCTV

D.   door sensor

E.   None of the choices.

2, You rely on what techniques to watch for unusual behaviors?

A.   surveillance

B.   investigation

C.   blockage

D.   detection

E.   None of the choices.

3, You use what kind of devices to sense changes that take place in an environment?

A.   surveillance

B.   investigation

C.   blockage

D. detection

E. None of the choices.

4, Monitoring live events is a measure of what nature?

A. proactive

B. reactive

C. descriptive

D. preventative

E. None of the choices.

5, Which of the following are major causes of physical losses that should be considered from a physical security perspective (choose all that apply):

A. Liquids

B. Organisms

C. Projectiles

D. Movement

E. None of the choices.

6, The main methods for protecting against power problems include (choose all that apply):

A.   UPS

B.   Power line conditioners

C.   Backup sources

D.   Power sensors

E.   None of the choices.

7, What is the main class of fires that involves common combustibles?

A.   Class I

B.   Class II

C.   Class III

D.   Class IV

E.   None of the choices.

8, What is the main class of fires that involves common electrical wires?

A.   Class A

B.   Class B

C.   Class C

D.   Class D

E.   None of the choices.

9, The technique of rummaging through commercial trash to collect useful business information is known as:

A.   Information diving

B.   Intelligence diving

C.   Identity diving

D.   System diving

E.   Program diving

F.   None of the choices.

10, ID cards should have clear pictures along with (choose all that apply):

A.   the employee's name.

B.   the organization's name.

C.   the employee's birth date.

D.   the employee's birth place.

E.   None of the choices.

11, What should be done to make identification of non-employees immediate?

A.   All employees are expected to use smart card.

B.   All employees are expected to wear identification.

C. All employees are expected to use password.

D. All employees are expected to use fingerprint for entrance.

E. None of the choices.

12, What should be set up in the main lobby of each building which has an open-access or open-door policy?

A. A firewall

B. A locked door

C. A bastion host

D. A security desk

E. None of the choices.

13, Drop-bolt locks should be installed with (choose all that apply):

A. wood frame

B. angle strike

C. metal frame

D. flat strike

E. None of the choices.

14, Cylinder removal would be a threat particularly worrisome for:

A. Exterior locks

B.   Interior locks

C.   Intrusion Sensor

D.   Smart Card Reader

E.   None of the choices.

15, Which of the following is the biggest limitation factor of a CCTV system?

A.   LENs

B.   Resolution

C.   Color depth

D.   Human

E.   None of the choices.

16, Which of the following makes an intruder's entry more difficult and give the appearance of a more secure facility?

A.   Fences

B.   Walls

C.   Cameras

D.   Sensors

E.   None of the choices.

17, Open ornamental fences are preferred over walls due to what reason?

A.   They are less costly to install.

B.   They are maintenance free.

C.   They do not block visibility.

D.   They have a stronger structure.

E.   None of the choices.

18, Which of the following correctly describe a latch bolt (choose all that apply):

A.   It has a beveled head.

B.   It has a spring bolt.

C.   The latch is spring loaded.

D.   It has a square faced bolt.

E.   None of the choices.

19, Which of the following correctly describe a dead bolt (choose all that apply):

A.   It has a beveled head.

B.   It has a spring bolt.

C.   The latch is spring loaded.

D.   It has a square faced bolt.

E.   None of the choices.

20, Which grade represents the MOST secure type of locksets?

A.   Grade I

B.   Grade II

C.   Grade III

D.   Grade IV

E.   None of the choices.

21, Fence disturbance sensor has a _____ nature.

A.   passive

B.   active

C.   None of the choices.

22, Bistatic sensor has a _____ nature.

A.   passive

B.   active

C.   None of the choices.

23, Video motion sensor has a _____ nature.

A.   passive

B.   active

C.   None of the choices.

24, Ultrasonic motion sensor has a _____ nature.

A.   passive

B.   active

C.   None of the choices.

25, You use duress alarms for signaling:

A.   general events

B.   external events

C.   internal events

D.   life threatening emergency

E.   None of the choices.

26, Photoelectric detectors generally respond _____ to smoke generated by smoldering fires.

A.   slower

B.   faster

C.   None of the choices.

27, UV frame detectors are sensitive to fires with (choose all that apply):

A.   hydrogen

B.   ammonia

C.   sulfur

D.   metals

E.   None of the choices.

28, Noise detector is more or less useless in the case of fire.

A.   True

B.   False

29, Which of the following are the valid classifications of fire in the US (choose all that apply):

A.   class A

B.   class B

C.   class C

D.   class D

E.   None of the choices.

30, Which of the following correctly describe the essence of vetting (choose all that apply):

A.   personal interview conducted under stress

B.   personal interview conducted under no stress

C.   personal interview conducted based on previous answers

D.   personal interview conducted based on new subjects

E.   None of the choices.

31, Why would you want to conduct an interview when vetting (choose all that apply):

A.   to impeach

B.   to observe

C.   to discover new leads

D.   to explore

E.   None of the choices.

32, The polygraph is a lie detector.

A.   true

B.   false

33, A polygraph may be of use during:

A.   investigation

B.   pretexting

C.   interrogation

D.   questionnaire

E.   None of the choices.

34, Chain-link fencing is mostly used for what purpose?

A.   perimeter fencing

B.   border fencing

C.   bastion fencing

D.   brick fencing

E.   None of the choices.

35, Integrity of the fence line may be jeopardized by:

A.   locks

B.   keypads

C.   openings at the bottom

D.   openings at the top

E.   None of the choices.

36, What is the primary alternative to a Chain-link fence?

A.   Masonry wall

B.   Point-link fence

C.   Brick-link fence

D. Bastion wall

E. None of the choices.

37, Which of the following are the valid categories of protective lighting (choose all that apply):

A. flood lighting

B. glare lighting

C. controlled lighting

D. movable lighting

E. None of the choices.

38, Which of the following is a real fast way of compromising a key system?

A. disclose the cut code numbers

B. disclose the manufacturer name

C. disclose the country of origin

D. disclose the size and complexity

E. None of the choices.

39, Generally speaking there are how many basic stages to a fire?

A. 2

B. 3

C.   4

D.   5

E.   6

F.   None of the choices.

40, Which of the following are the valid types of manual fire alarm stations (choose all that apply):

A.   single action

B.   double action

C.   triple action

D.   zero action

E.   None of the choices.

41, Heat detectors may be classified as (choose all that apply):

A.   fixed temperature

B.   rate-of-rise

C.   rate-of-fire

D.   rate-of-spread

E.   None of the choices.

42, What is the most commonly used perimeter structural barrier?

A.   Chain link fence

B.   Grill

C.   Culvert

D.   Drapper

E.   None of the choices.

43, A chain link fence should have a minimum height of:

A.   7 ft

B.   6 ft

C.   5 ft

D.   12 ft

E.   16 ft

44, When used as a barrier, walls should be of (choose all that apply):

A.   masonry block

B.   brick

C.   wire

D.   grill

E.   None of the choices.

45, When using grills with windows, which of the following is true?

A. You should have the grills set back from glass at least 20 inches

B. You should have the grills set back from glass at least 18 inches

C. You should have the grills set back from glass at least 12 inches

D. You should have the grills set back from glass at least 4 inches

E. None of the choices.

46, What kind of glass will not shatter when stroked?

A. Grill glass

B. Metallic glass

C. Spinlter-proof glass

D. Wire mesh glass

E. None of the choices.

47, Protective lighting should NOT be used in conjunction with:

A. guard posts

B. foot patrols

C. fences

D. alarm systems

E. None of the choices.

48, Which of the following is true concerning hallway lighting?

A.   A minimum 50% light visibility must be maintained

B.   A minimum 75% light visibility must be maintained

C.   A minimum 90% light visibility must be maintained

D.   Complete darkness is allowed only at mid night

E.   None of the choices.

49, Ventilation ducts should be kept to a minimum in areas with confidential data stored on open shelves.

A.   True

B.   False

50, Concrete used for vault construction should be (choose all that apply):

A.   monolithic

B.   poured and cast in place

C.   5 inches thick at least

D.   None of the choices.

51, A deadbolt has no spring action.

A.   True

B.   False

52, With pin tumbler, what determines security level?

A.   The number of pins

B.   The angle of the pin

C.   The width of the pin

D.   None of the choices.

53, An interlocking strike works only with rim-mounted latchbolt.

A.   True

B.   False

54, Windows is the most common point of entry into the building.

A.   True

B.   False

55, An awning window opens:

A.   inward

B.   outward

56, A casement window has a sash hinged on:

A.   the top

B.   the bottom

C.   the side

D.   None of the choices.

57, Concerning the A-B-C-D method, A stands for:

A.   AIDS

B.   ADVANCED

C.   ACCUMULATED

D.   ATOMIC

E.   None of the choices.

58, Chain link fencing has been the product of choice for security fencing for over 60 years because of which of the following characteristics (choose all that apply):

A.   strength

B.   corrosion resistance

C.   see thru capabilities

D.   ease of installation

E.   None of the choices.

59. Material specifications for chain link fence are listed in which of the following (choose all that apply):

A.   CLFMI

B.   ASTM

C.   Federal Specification RR-F-191 K/GEN

D.   None of the choices.

60, The framework for a chain link fence consists of (choose all that apply):

A.   line posts

B.   end posts

C.   corner posts

D.   gateposts

E.   None of the choices.

61, The omission of a rail at the top of the fence is desirable due to what reason?

A.   it makes the fence more difficult to climb.

B.   it makes the fence stronger

C.   it makes the fence water proof

D.   it makes the fence less costly to make

E.   None of the choices.

62, Color polymer coated chain link fabric has what primary advantage?

A.   It enhances reliability.

B.   It enhances strength.

C.   It enhances durability.

D.   It enhances visibility.

E.   None of the choices.

63, A Class V rated security container can afford how many man minutes against surreptitious entry?

A.   30

B.   10

C.   20

D.   60

E.   None of the choices.

64, A Class V rated security container can afford how many man minutes against lock manipulation?

A.   30

B.   10

C.   20

D.   60

E.   None of the choices.

65, A Class III rated security container can afford how many man minutes against radiological attack?

A.   30

B.   10

C.   20

D.   60

E.   None of the choices.

Mock Test Answers

1. A B C D   Physical security is often a critical part of security policy. Related access control includes practices such as restricting entrance to authorized personnel only. One may implement physical access control through a human guard or a mechanical lock or any other fancy ways, such as using CCTV to monitor physical activities of the staff, or deploying door sensor to detect the opening of doors. You do need to know the difference: you rely on surveillance techniques to watch for unusual behaviors. On the other hand, you use detecting devices to sense changes that take place in an environment. Monitoring live events is a preventative measure, while recording events is a detective one.

2. A   Physical security is often a critical part of security policy. Related access control includes practices such as restricting entrance to authorized personnel only. One may implement physical access control through a human guard or a mechanical lock or any other fancy ways, such as using CCTV to monitor physical activities of the staff, or deploying door sensor to detect the opening of doors. You do need to know the difference: you rely on surveillance techniques to watch for unusual behaviors. On the other hand, you use detecting devices to sense changes that take place in an environment. Monitoring live events is a preventative measure, while recording events is a detective one.

3. D   Physical security is often a critical part of security policy. Related access control includes practices such as restricting entrance to authorized personnel only. One may implement physical access control through a human guard or a mechanical lock or any other fancy ways, such as using CCTV to monitor physical activities of the staff, or deploying door sensor to detect the opening of doors. You do need to know the difference: you rely on surveillance techniques to watch for unusual behaviors. On the other hand, you use detecting devices to sense changes that take place in an environment. Monitoring live events is a preventative measure, while recording events is a detective one.

4. D   Physical security is often a critical part of security policy. Related access control includes practices such as restricting entrance to authorized personnel only. One may implement physical access control through a human guard or a mechanical lock or any other fancy ways, such as using CCTV to monitor physical activities of the staff, or deploying door sensor to detect the opening of doors. You do need to know the difference: you rely on surveillance techniques to watch for unusual behaviors. On the other hand, you use detecting devices to sense changes that take place in

an environment. Monitoring live events is a preventative measure, while recording events is a detective one.

5. A B C D   Physical security is way more than just malicious acts conducted by hackers. It has been said that there are seven major causes of physical losses that should be considered from a physical security perspective. They include Temperate (Sunlight, fire, freezing, heat), Gases (War gases, vapors, humidity, dry air, smoke, smog), Liquids (Water, chemicals), Organisms (People, animals, viruses, bacteria), Projectiles (Meteors, cars and trucks, bullets, tornados), Movement (Collapse, shearing, shaking, earthquakes), and Energy Anomalies (Surges or power failures, static, radiation, magnets). Some of them are less likely in a modern environment. Still, you have to prepare for them – you may want to address them in your physical security plan.

6. A B C   Pay particular attention to the issues of power outage and fire suppression. The main methods for protecting against power problems include UPS, Power line conditioners and backup sources.

7. E   The four main classes of fires are Class A - Common combustibles; Class B - Liquid fires; Class C - Electrical equipment and wires; and Class D - Combustible metals. Halon is best for handling Class C fire but is no longer legal due to environmental issues.

8. C   The four main classes of fires are Class A - Common combustibles; Class B - Liquid fires; Class C - Electrical equipment and wires; and Class D - Combustible metals. Halon is best for handling Class C fire but is no longer legal due to environmental issues.

9. A   Dumpster diving in the form of information diving describes the practice of rummaging through commercial trash to find useful information such as files, letters, memos, passwords …etc.

10. A   ID cards should have clear pictures along with the employee's name. The institution's name may not necessarily be placed on the card though.

11. B   All employees are expected to wear identification. This makes identification of non-employees immediate.

12. D A security desk should be set up in the main lobby of each building which has an open-access or open-door policy.

13. A B C D Exterior locks should conform to the following: i, Lock cylinders should be pick-resistant; ii, Drop-bolt locks should be installed with the proper strike: wood frame, angle strike; metal frame, flat strike; and iii, there should be metal guard places to prevent cylinder removal.

14. A Exterior locks should conform to the following: i, Lock cylinders should be pick-resistant; ii, Drop-bolt locks should be installed with the proper strike: wood frame, angle strike; metal frame, flat strike; and iii, there should be metal guard places to prevent cylinder removal.

15. D CCTV system will become ineffective if those responsible for monitoring the cameras are overworked, poorly trained, tired or distracted.

16. A Fences make an intruder's entry more difficult and give the appearance of a more secure facility. Open ornamental fences are preferred over walls as they do not block visibility.

17. C Fences make an intruder's entry more difficult and give the appearance of a more secure facility. Open ornamental fences are preferred over walls as they do not block visibility.

18. A B C (Muuss and Rabern, pg 177)

19. D (Muuss and Rabern, pg 177)

20. A (Muuss and Rabern, pg 180)

21. A (Muuss and Rabern, pg 206)

22. B (Muuss and Rabern, pg 208)

23. A (Muuss and Rabern, pg 208)

24. B (Muuss and Rabern, pg 211)

25. D (Muuss and Rabern, pg 213)

26. B   (Muuss and Rabern, pg 229)

27. A B C D   (Muuss and Rabern, pg 231)

28. B   (Muuss and Rabern, pg 232)

29. A B C D   (Muuss and Rabern, pg 235)

30. A C   (Muuss and Rabern, pg 244)

31. A B C D   (Muuss and Rabern, pg 244)

32. B   (Muuss and Rabern, pg 244)

33. C   (Muuss and Rabern, pg 247)

34. A   (Fay, 146)

35. C   (Fay, 146)

36. A   (Fay, 146)

37. A B C D   (Fay, 147)

38. A   (Fay, 156)

39. D   (Muuss and Rabern, pg 223)

40. A B (Muuss and Rabern, pg 224)

41. A B (Muuss and Rabern, pg 226)

42. A   (Roper, pg 57)

43. A (Roper, pg 57)

44. A B (Roper, pg 61)

45. D (Roper, pg 63)

46. D (Roper, pg 67)

47. E (Roper, pg 73)

48. A (Roper, pg 75)

49. A (Roper, pg 89)

50. A B (Roper, pg 87)

51. A (Roper, pg 104)

52. A (Roper, pg 104)

53. B (Roper, pg 106)

54. B (Roper, pg 115)

55. A (Roper, pg 115)

56. C (Roper, pg 115)

57. A (Roper, pg 54)

58. A B C D Chain link fencing has been the product of choice for security fencing for over 60 years because of its strength, corrosion resistance, "see thru capabilities", ease of installation, versatility, variety of product selection and value.

59. A B C Material specifications for chain link fence are listed in the following: (CLFMI) Chain Link Manufacturers Institute Product Manual; ASTM (American Society of Testing Materials) Volume 01.06; Federal Specification RR-F-191 K/GEN, 14 May 1990; ASTM F 1553

60. A B C D The framework for a chain link fence consists of the line posts, end posts, corner posts, gateposts, and if required top, mid, bottom or brace rail.

61. A The omission of a rail at the top of the fence eliminates a handhold thus making the fence more difficult to climb.

62. D Color polymer coated chain link fabric enhances visibility, especially at night.

63. A (Roper, pg 139)

64. C (Roper, pg 139)

65. C (Roper, pg 139)

All orders come with LIFE TIME FREE UPDATES. When you find a newer version of the purchased product all you need to do is to email us and we will send you the updated version BY EMAIL free of charge.

Our email address: Michael@examreview.net

Made in the USA
Lexington, KY
14 September 2012